CULTURE FOX

CULTURE FOX

HOW TO CULTIVATE A LASTING CULTURE.
MY PATH FROM HAIR STYLIST
TO INTERNATIONAL CEO.

LOREAN CAIRNS

CULTURE FOX

*How to Cultivate a Lasting Culture. My Path
From Hair Stylist to International CEO.*

ISBN 978-1-5445-0232-8 *Hardcover*

978-1-5445-0231-1 *Paperback*

978-1-5445-0230-4 *Ebook*

To my team and partners. Never had I dreamed of being in this position, and now because of all of you, I could never dream of anything less. Onward and upward.

CONTENTS

___

INTRODUCTION

———

Hi! I'm Lorean Cairns, founder of Fox and Jane Salon. But more than that, I am a stylist and entrepreneur with a passion for developing and nurturing managers into leaders, and salons into places where both stylists and clients really want to be. My reason for doing so is simple: I want every salon owner, leader, stylist, and client to have the *ultimate experience.*

There are plenty of negative clichés about hair stylists. Our industry has earned its less-than-stellar reputation, and I've been around long enough to know that sometimes these clichés are true. But I also know they don't *have* to be. Your salon doesn't have to be one of the 80 percent of salons that are 2 percent profitable—or that close their doors within three years. In fact, those stats can be changed significantly if salon owners focus on blowing the preconceived notions about their business culture out of the water.

Over the years, I've worked in a variety of environments (more on that in a few minutes). I've seen and experienced both extremes of the salon culture and everything in between. I've seen what works and what doesn't. Somewhere along the way, I started thinking about the fact that no salon—or any other business, for that matter—should have to settle for a less-than-amazing workplace culture.

That is why I wrote this book—to help you turn your business into a place people *want* to work, where they feel safe and confident in their ability to excel in their field, and where clients/customers want to come because they know they are valued for who they are—not just for their contribution to your bottom line.

Within the pages of this book, you are going to discover why it is important to make the work environment a safe place to fail, how to hire the right person to train—not the right person for the job—how to correct a problem correctly, how to make standards instead of rules, how to make and meet business goals, and a whole lot more.

I am aware of the fact that there are countless books available about running a successful business. But not all of them will work for businesses where customer relationships are as essential as they are in the salon industry (as well as many others). And finally, not all of them were written by a small business owner who went from scraping a few thousand dollars together in 2011, to opening my first salon, to owning a fourteen-million-dollar company with nine salons and 150 employees in 2018.

My journey has not always been easy. I've struggled often, and many times I didn't have the answer. During those times, one thing remained the same—I dug in harder, supported, cheered, and coached. I listened and observed, and one day at a time, I found clarity. I created systems, and allowed others the opportunity to lead. When they failed, I didn't scold—I helped change narratives and grew some more, until one day I realized that helping others is what serves me. That is how I came to write this book. For me, teaching you how to make your business the best it can be *from the inside out* is the reward for all my efforts. If you are serious about being successful as a leader and as a business owner, I'd love to help.

.

THE "HUMBLE BEGINNING" STORY IS MY STORY

A person who is appreciated will always do (and be) more than is expected of them.

—UNKNOWN

The "country mouse makes good" story is about as cliché as clichés come in regard to stylists. I get it. But in my case, that was just what happened. I was raised in small-town Colorado—a town of less than twenty thousand—in a house on a dirt road. As the youngest of four children in a sleepy little mountain town, I certainly never dreamed my life would take me on this adventure. I'm grateful for my time in Colorado; I learned so much there and wouldn't trade it. Whether I knew it at the time or not, it prepared me for my journey as a business owner in New York City.

Had I not grown up in Durango, I wouldn't have worked for my first mentor, Lenore Brieger. It is from Lenore that I first came to learn the importance of workplace culture. And had I not learned *that*, Fox and Jane probably wouldn't even exist.

Anyway, after graduating from high school, I enrolled in cosmetology school. It was pretty much "love at first sight" for me. I knew being a stylist was my dream job *and* that I happened to be good at it.

After I graduated from cosmetology school, I went to work for Lenore at the Lemonhead Salon—one of or perhaps *the* best decision I've made in my life.

Lenore made her stylists feel like they had a vested interest in the salon—not so much from the dollars-and-cents perspective, but from an employer-employee perspective. You knew Lenore cared about you as a person and as a professional. But more than that, she also taught me how to care about those things, too.

Some other key things I learned from Lenore were the following:

- She taught me that who I am as a person reflects who I am as a professional and vice versa.
- She taught me how to handle conflict in a healthy, mature manner, guaranteeing positive resolution.
- She taught me how to be personable with clients without letting them monopolize my time doing things such as throwing off my schedule, costing me bookings, or crossing my professional boundaries.
- She taught me how to do GREAT hair.
- She taught me that the workplace culture is the most important thing about a business.
- She taught me to believe in myself and to put myself out there so other people would believe in me, too.

When you worked for Lenore, you wanted to come to work. The fact that I worked there seven years and that during that time there was next to no turnover is something you just don't find in the salon industry very often. That alone should give you an idea of just how great an employer and businesswoman Lenore is. A Lemonhead stylist was a confident, happy, well-trained, and highly respected stylist. What's not to love about that, right? You knew what to expect and what was expected of you. You also knew Lenore had your back—always. She never had a problem sticking up for her team because she'd trained us—she knew what and whom she was backing.

After seven years, I realized I was ready to take everything

I'd learned out for a spin. I had my heart set on New York City and was ready to make the leap. I didn't just want to move around the corner or even across the state. No, I was like Lauren Conrad of *The Hills* heading off to her internship at *Teen Vogue* in Los Angeles. I knew I was up for the challenge, and even though I didn't know what lay ahead, I was dead set on starting this adventure. So I did. I sold my car, emptied my bank account, packed all my worldly possessions into four suitcases, and hopped on a plane to New York City.

Why New York City? Life in NYC seemed so impossibly glamorous. I was ready for variety and anonymity (after growing up in a small town), and I knew New York would deliver. Also, I just started to follow my gut, and my gut said, "Go to New York City!" I was luckier than most people, though. I had a friend already living there who helped me land an interview for my first job about a week after I arrived. I arrived at the interview full of confidence in myself as a person and confidence in my skills as a stylist. They must have liked what they saw—to some extent, anyway—because I got the job.

This job wasn't your typical first job in the big city either. It was in an extremely elite celebrity salon on Fifth Avenue—next door to Trump Tower. Jennifer Lopez, Jessica Simpson, and Beyoncé were just a few of the regulars.

This seemed like the ultimate job for a stylist; I was over the moon with excitement. How much more could a girl ask for, especially being the new kid on the block, right? Wrong...and wrong again. The atmosphere was absolutely toxic from day one! But because I knew how fortunate I was to get the job, I did my best to make it work. I have to tell you, though, that I was utterly and completely miserable. I was losing myself and my passion for my work. And for what?

Thankfully, I had the willpower and enough self-respect to walk away. I will say, however, that while what I learned in my brief time there wasn't positive, per se, it was valuable. Working in that environment introduced me to my first highly toxic work environment—every negative cliché you can imagine in one place.

But this was supposed to be the best of the best? Experiencing it firsthand taught me that it was not the way I wanted to spend my career or how I wanted others to have to spend theirs.

I learned how it felt to be disrespected by your employer, and I can tell you it doesn't feel good. It's awful. When I worked at the Lemonhead, respect wasn't an option. You gave it and you got it. The end. In this salon, employees were greatly disrespected and undervalued.

I learned that pleasing the client at all costs isn't worth the cost of your self-respect.

I learned that customer service needs to be a little personal. Otherwise, it's not service but, rather, *subservience*. For example, in that salon, assistants would do whatever it took to give the clients in this shop whatever they wanted: lunch, hand massages, gourmet coffee—you name it, they got it. But these things were delivered robot-fashion. We were told to treat them with a superficial attitude that might be best described as "hero worship." Personal interaction was strictly forbidden. I was actually criticized for my warm, bubbly personality, and directed to speak only when spoken to. Not because I didn't have professional social boundaries, but because staff was not permitted to shine in this environment.

So like I said, I was miserable. This was not what I had in mind when I moved to New York, so I walked away. I knew I had a lot to offer. I just needed to find the right salon.

Unfortunately, the next salon I worked at wasn't the right one either. It was located in the West Village, in a notoriously trendy and upscale part of Lower Manhattan. The problem there was that the owner didn't believe in marketing. He believed our work should speak for itself.

I agree that your work should speak for itself, but it

shouldn't be the only thing talking. If a business doesn't market itself, your work won't have anyone to speak to. It was because he didn't market the salon that I didn't make any money. I existed on a college student diet of ramen, and peanut butter and jelly sandwiches. So...

I soon found myself looking for my third job in less than a year. I had worked at Lemonhead for seven years, meaning that this situation was completely unfamiliar territory.

Job number three was a salon in the East Village. The salon was small and outdated, and the owner took little interest in making improvements or even meeting basic standards. Looking on the bright side, though, the other girls in the shop and I were a great fit. Almost instantly, we were working together, and playing together, too.

Our chemistry and our energy started catching the attention of our clients, who then started recommending us to their friends. Not only that, but people started walking in off the street to get their hair done because they could feel the good vibes coming from the shop.

The energy the other two girls and I shared was great, but my intuition told me that it could be even better than it was. If the positive energy we shared was channeled properly, we could easily take that salon to levels that weren't even on the owner's radar.

After giving it some serious thought, I went to the owner of the salon and asked him if he would consider making me the salon's manager since he was notoriously absent. He told me he didn't think I should bother with being just a manager—that I should open my own shop. He said he thought I would make an even better salon *owner.*

My own salon? Now *that* got me thinking!

I decided I owed it to myself to at least investigate the possibilities. The more research I did, the more convinced I became that owning my own salon was doable. My research also connected me with Billy, a marketing guru and great friend. He suggested that we team up—me running the salon and him handling the marketing. Fox and Jane was born!

Our first location: lower east side of Manhattan. It was small but pretty. The "pretty" was courtesy of Bobby Berk, who is a dear friend, an amazing designer, and now one of the stars on *Queer Eye* on Netflix Life. One of the girls from the shop I left came with me to the new Fox and Jane. The other one, who during this time had gone home to LA, decided to come back and work for me, too. The three of us were together again. I told them, though, that if we were going to do this, we were going to do it better than anyone else had ever done it before.

We did, and we still are.

IT'S YOUR TURN

THE "HUMBLE BEGINNING" STORY IS MY STORY, TOO

———

I once heard someone say that we are the product of our raising; meaning, you live what you've learned. Both statements are true, but both are also relative statements. In other words, what we take from our experiences and how we use them depends on us—we are the author of our own story.

I've told you my story, so now it's time for you to tell yours. Use the next couple of pages to write your story. It doesn't have to be anything fancy. You're not going for a Pulitzer, a feature in the *Wall Street Journal*, or even a trade publication you read cover to cover. This is for you.

By writing your story, you will be able to reflect on the who, what, and why of your professional journey. In doing so, you will be better able to assess your progress, set goals that are both challenging and attainable, and decide whether or not you are doing everything you can to be your best professional self.

Feel free to use the following questions as a sort of outline and start writing.

- Where did you come from?
- What did you want to be when you grew up?
- Who did you want to be like? Why?
- Who didn't you want to be like? Why?
- What was your first job?
- What did you learn from that job?
- How has your education helped bring you to where you are today?
- What have you learned along the way that could never be taught in a classroom?
- What jobs have you had up to this point?
- What did you learn from each of them?
- Who is your mentor(s), and why?
- Why did you choose the profession you are in?
- What contributions have you made along the way?
- What contributions do you want to make to your profession?

CULTURE IS KING

———

We are not a team because we work together. We are a team because we respect, trust, and care for each other.

—VALA AFSHAR

When I told the girls we were going to do it better than anyone else ever had, they already basically knew what "it" was. They knew because they had been listening, watching, and working toward it for months—since I'd first walked through the door of the salon where we met. They knew the "it" I was talking about meant what Fox and Jane would offer their employees and clients:

- The high-end level of professionalism and product perfection they expect from a salon on Fifth Avenue. No details are left unattended. The finish level of services provided is always top-notch. We go above and beyond in our effort to serve the client.

- Conversations are fun, well-mannered, respectful, and most importantly, we get to be ourselves with our clients; yet, there is always an appropriate balance between being friendly and professional.
- We are warm, courteous, and caring, but we are in control of our business. No lines are crossed, yet clients are made to feel a part of the salon's community-like culture.
- Clients know they are our top priority. They feel welcome and special. They know they will be listened to. We are solicitous without sacrificing our self-respect.
- The salon has a cozy, yet high-energy, sense of community and diversity. Truly, everyone is welcome here. You can see and feel the camaraderie among the stylists. It has a family-like atmosphere because we are extended family.

My first (semi-)long-term goal going into this whole thing was to make $21,000 a month. It makes me laugh a little now. In doing so, I would be able to take home a couple of thousand dollars over and above my commissions. This, I figured, would make me very happy and confirm that I had made the right move in opening the salon. I met and exceeded that goal in only four months.

Within six months of opening our first Fox and Jane, we were booked up for the whole month. We were then able to hire another stylist (more on that later). Much of the thanks for our rapid success goes to Billy, who was doing an amazing job of marketing by way of digital marketing. We began generating online reviews, calling on some PR professionals we knew to give us some press in all the right places, and of course, by word of mouth.

We grew quickly—so quickly that less than a year after opening the door, we decided to branch out and open a second location. After looking around for just the right place, we decided on a building located about fifteen blocks away (uptown). Opening the second location also opened up the issue of how to make sure both salons upheld the principles of workplace culture I insisted on so adamantly. After giving it some careful thought, I put one of the stylists who had originally come with me in the position of salon leader at Fox and Jane "number one." I took the other stylist with me to Fox and Jane "number two." I spent about eight months training her as lead stylist for this location.

From there, Billy and I headed out west to San Diego. A friend of his had a salon that was in financial trouble and was closing her shop. Billy suggested to her that we go out and reopen the shop using our name and business model and hire her as a manager.

This was without a doubt the best, and worst, thing I have ever done. Never have I learned more about business and about myself than I did from this situation.

From the beginning, it was obvious we did not share the same values or vision for the salon. From this experience, I learned I will never again work with or hire someone who doesn't share my core business values. If these are not shared, the culture of a workplace can never be healthy.

We also did not agree on the fact that no matter whose idea gets you there, the end result should be a great product. The former owner, now lead stylist-in-training wanted to be the star or to be given credit for the success of the turnaround. Stardom doesn't appeal to me. Fox and Jane is the star, not one or two people. In short, she consistently chose to challenge me rather than collaborate with me.

But I cannot lay all the blame on her. I was lacking in clarity on my end. My communication skills were lacking, and I didn't always know how to express a change or how to follow through on a vision...across the country. I was learning. I still am.

In the end, the owner couldn't come to terms with the fact that the salon wouldn't be successful unless she applied the Fox and Jane business model, so she left. Billy and I hung in there, though, and I'm glad we did, because Fox and Jane in San Diego has been, and continues to be, highly successful.

After San Diego, things just kept growing. We were also getting a lot of attention from other people in the industry. Other salon owners couldn't help but notice that what we were doing was working well.

One of those salon owners was my friend and former coworker in Colorado; Brittany was tired and lonely as a sole proprietor. She was just getting started and didn't have anyone to mentor her or to bounce ideas off. Her business was small but going well, so she reached out to me via a popular social network we all know and love. I was more than happy to answer a few questions for her and give her a bit of advice. But it soon became apparent that she wanted and needed more than I was willing to just give away.

I know that may sound harsh to some, but it isn't. Think about it—if someone comes up with an invention or an idea that they are confident others will want to buy into, they aren't just going to give the idea away. Well, that's how it was with me. It was obvious I had a formula for business that works. So at that point, I tactfully told Brittany I couldn't offer her any more advice, *but* if she was interested, we could merge our skills and really grow her business. One thing quickly led to another, and the end result is that Brittany is now my business partner.

Oh, and her shop in Colorado is doing GREAT as a Fox

and Jane Salon. In fact, she has just opened her second location in Denver, Colorado, in less than two years of partnership!

All of this goes to show that the success of Fox and Jane is not just because of me. Fox and Jane's growth and success is because of what we do *together.* I don't manage. I lead. I lead the stylists in charge of Fox and Jane locations. They then *lead* (not manage) the other stylists. And they, in turn, lead me to be a strong and consistent leader. It is one big circle, one that produces big results.

When I talk to managers, I get the feeling that they are important. When I talk to leaders, I get the feeling that I am important.

—UNKNOWN

We have created a culture where the main principle is leading each other to be and do our best. Sounds simple, I know, but that's really it. We are constantly leading each other to live that age-old golden rule—to treat others the way we want to be treated—and to be the top-notch version of ourselves professionally every single day.

I understand that as a leader, I cannot lose sight of the fact that my business is more important to me than always being right. It may sound corny, but business is my spiritual journey. It's where I learn, dig deep, and set goals, and it has helped me to become the best version of myself. Fox and Jane has empowered me to be a more thoughtful, evaluative, communicative, and giving person.

As Fox and Jane has grown, I've been humbled by the telltale signs of our success. For example:

- Being at a dinner party with a stranger who comments that they keep hearing all sorts of wonderful things about Fox and Jane.
- Getting so booked that even our new hires book four weeks in advance the day they start (with no following of their own). People just know that if they are a Fox and Jane stylist, they can be trusted.
- Getting hundreds of applications when we open a position. Stylists want to work with us because our culture's reputation is unprecedented.
- Reading our Yelp reviews still makes me cry. I set out to make a positive, accessible place for clients and staff alike, and it has grown so much bigger than I ever imagined.
- Being referenced in *Allure*, *Seventeen*, *Redbook*, and other publications.
- Seeing my clients whose hair I haven't done in five years still coming to Fox and Jane stylists.
- In 2017, we had fifty-six full-time hair stylists in our NYC area. Not one of them quit within a full calendar year. Not one!

My business principles obviously have some merit, because in February 2018, we opened our ninth location and are on track to make more than one million dollars in revenue per month by the end of this year. Some days, it still seems like a dream. In almost seven short but crazy-busy years, I've gone from a girl with no money and a passion for being a great stylist to a woman passing on her passion for being a great stylist and the CEO of a fourteen-million-dollar business with more than 150 extended Fox and Jane family members. Wow!

I am also a businesswoman who has realized that I have a business platform that can be used to help you obtain your own level of success. And being the natural-born leader that I am, I can't help but want to lead you to it.

IT'S YOUR TURN

CULTURE IS KING

———

The following are a series of questions about your workplace and the culture you create there. Take a moment to reflect and respond to them in your own time.

1. How would you describe the culture of your workplace?

2. In what ways does the culture of your workplace encourage employees to strive to be their best? To conduct themselves in a professional manner? To be loyal to your company?

3. In what ways does the culture of your workplace *discourage* employees from doing the things listed in question 2?

4. What improvements need to be made to your work culture?

5. Describe the healthiest work culture you have experienced. How did it affect you directly?

6. Describe the most toxic work culture you have experienced. How did it affect you directly?

7. What changes are you going to make to your company's work culture?

8. How are you going to introduce these changes?

9. What, if any, resistance do you anticipate in making these changes?

10. How will you handle any resistance that may present itself?

11. After making these improvements, what changes would you hope to see in your employees and in the overall operation of your business?

12. Select two or three businesses (not necessarily in your profession) that seem to have everything under control. Ask the business owner how they maintain a positive and productive job culture. What did you learn that can enhance your ability to create the best possible culture in your workplace?

EFFECTIVE LEADERSHIP

———

The function of leadership is to produce more leaders...not more followers.

—RALPH NADER

So many people think leadership is about being at the top of a pyramid. I don't. I truly believe leadership is actually about being at the bottom of a pyramid. As a leader, you are the stepping stone that every journey begins with. People in your organization climb up onto your back to get higher, and in turn, this serves the bigger picture for your business.

LEADERSHIP VERSUS MANAGEMENT

When I Googled the definition of a manager, the following definitions were the first to pop up:

- A person responsible for controlling or administering all or part of a company or similar organization.
- A person who controls the activities, business dealings, and other aspects of the career of another person.

But when I look at the definition for a leader, it just says: *to lead*. (What happened to that rule about not using the word you are defining in the definition?) So I went to the trusty thesaurus on my laptop to see what words could be used in place of *leader*. Here are a few I found:

- Trailblazer
- Frontrunner
- Organizer
- Chief
- Director
- Guide
- Mentor
- Head
- Adviser
- Supervisor

I don't know about you, but I'd much rather be guided, directed, mentored, and supervised than controlled.

No, I take that back—I *do* know about you, because in the seven years I've been at the helm of Fox and Jane, I've seen the transformation in stylists who come from an atmosphere of being managed to using our leadership philosophy. And I can tell you, it is always a positive transformation.

Leadership is essential, but it is only effective when people are following. When you lead rather than manage, you are sending your stylists/employees the message that you value *their* work. You value *their* capabilities and ideas. You value *them*. Leadership also allows everyone to be an active and respected participant in the business. And why shouldn't they be? We're all a necessary part of it. From the parking attendant to the president, from the custodian to the CEO—we all need each other. We are a team.

That's why, for the next few pages, we are going to focus on what makes a good leader and why leading (as opposed to managing) is the way to go. We will also look at a few examples of what happens when a business doesn't provide solid leadership. That way, you will see for yourself what a difference it truly makes when you organize, lead, guide, and mentor, instead of controlling and administrating.

LESSON ONE: WHAT HAPPENS WHEN LEADERS STOP LEADING

In 1987, an optometrist by the name of Ben Israel went

to the executives of Sears and Roebuck, and Walmart's founder, Sam Walton, with an innovative business model. His idea was to put vision centers in retail stores, giving people the ability to get their eyes examined and purchase vision wear as easily as they would a new dress, a coffee maker, or a gallon of milk.

Both retailers saw the practicality of the idea as well as the potential for a substantial amount of money to be made. Within a few short years, Israel had opened stores in more than two hundred Walmart locations and dozens of Sears stores (this was before Sears crashed).

Things were going well...until they weren't. In other words, as long as the company was following the original business model, which included a leadership philosophy, all was well. But the business started growing so quickly that Mr. Israel started cutting corners when it came to training the people he depended on to lead each new store. It was also around this time that Sam Walton died. Sam's death meant a complete turnover in the leadership of Walmart as well. They were highly capable, but driven solely by dollars and cents.

Mr. Israel's negligence in training store leaders to operate according to the principles the business had been built on, combined with the impersonal new team at the helm of Walmart, started affecting every aspect of the business.

Both groups of people had a management mindset (control) instead of a leadership mindset (follow me).

By 1994, Mr. Israel and his company were on the brink of personal and financial disaster. Israel was pushed out with basically nothing to show for his innovation, success, and formerly respected leadership skills.

Some of you are probably thinking, "Wait! There are still vision centers in Walmart, so what's the problem?"

You are right—Walmart stores still have vision centers. But that doesn't mean they are operating as well as they could be. It doesn't mean the culture of the work environment is what it should and could be. It doesn't mean customers are getting the level of service and attention they should and could be.

Now, please know that I am *not picking on* Walmart and I am *not saying* their vision centers are doomed. There are a number of businesses with healthy bottom lines that run on management principles instead of leadership principles. What I *am* saying is that when they deviated from a business model based on *leadership* rather than management, they imploded and had to be rebuilt from the bottom up.

When a person feels respected and valued, they respect and value you right back. In other words, the employee who is made to feel valued and respected will be more loyal to you, make their best effort, and will be a walking, talking billboard for the business...in a good way. And with *those* things in place, your business is in a position to flourish.

The Attributes of an Effective Leader

Effective leaders think about their business from a *culture point of view*, meaning their number one priority is to instill, and insist on, a healthy atmosphere—one that is healthy for employees and clients. Effective leaders know that if the work culture is thriving, the business is in the best possible position to prosper.

But what makes a leader effective?

An effective leader is a leader who:

- **Inspires.** Effective leaders inspire those around them. They accomplish this through the vision they set forth, providing a picture of the future toward which everyone is then motivated to strive. Their **passion is contagious**, and their **energy is evident** in every task they undertake. Their dedication and commitment to the company and those they are leading serve to motivate—not just to do as their leaders do but to also believe that what they are working toward is within their reach. Effective leaders **use themes, mottoes, and symbols to inspire** staff members and to **maintain their focus on shared objectives.**

- **Develops Relationships.** Leadership is about relationships—not friendships, per se, but relationships (more on that a bit later). As much as effective leaders focus on improving instruction, they also invest time in cultivating personal connections. Good leaders listen to staff members and recognize important issues in their lives, talking with them not just as colleagues or employees but also as people. An added bonus to developing these relationships is that building these connections allows you to uncover an individual's talents and strengths, which in turn allows leaders to get the most out of their staff—to guide and mentor staff members toward reaching their full potential.
- **Monitors Climate.** Simply put, effective leaders know what is happening in the building, even if they aren't in the building—not in a controlling way, mind you, but in such a way that they are never caught off-guard when a problem arises. They are conscious of hidden problems, emerging problems, and public problems. This allows for a proactive approach that may be as simple as anticipating supply needs and

room arrangements, or may be as serious as observing and addressing instructional and personal issues. Effective leaders will see it coming and be able to dilute a problem or even keep it from surfacing. This is possible because effective leaders are aware of the web of relationships connecting staff members, teams, and departments. They stay on top of concerns and complaints connected to operations. They know how to prioritize without minimizing an issue's importance to staff members.

- **Nurtures.** So much of what effective leaders do could be defined as nurturing. Wise leaders cultivate their staff members' leadership skills—both to ensure support in carrying out and sustaining change, *and* to establish a network of rising leaders to fill future positions. Effective leaders make sure no one is left behind. They pick up those who fall, lend an ear or a shoulder to those who need support, and generally reenergize staff members and prepare them for the day ahead. Good leaders may not *enjoy* the company of all of their staff members, but they are sure to demonstrate care and concern for each and every one of them through their words and actions. They avoid judgment and focus on needs and progress. Effective leaders know that kindness always matters.

- **Sets the Culture.** Not all leaders have the opportunity to create a culture from scratch. Most inherit it from previous leaders. This can be a good thing...or a bad thing. Whether establishing a new culture or enhancing the existing one, effective leaders put in place norms and practices that include *their* **choices and methods in hiring, promoting, or not renewing contracts** for staff. They must do so to ensure productive collaboration, data analysis, staff development, and professional dialogues.

- **Maintains Visibility.** A leader I know told me how he had solicited feedback from staff members on what they believed to be the positive and negative aspects of his leadership. He told me that one of the most common observations made was that he was not visible enough. He seemed to be around only when things were either really good or really bad. Effective leaders are **visible on a regular basis.** They are the face of the team. They mingle not only during coaching or training but also during day-to-day routines. They interject themselves in an appropriate manner into interactions with guests/clients, and they find time to connect with the team each day through conversation—not necessarily work related. Visibility on this level helps leaders stay in touch with people's needs, wants, and concerns; it also demonstrates that they are working shoulder to shoulder.

LESSON TWO: LEADERS STILL HAVE TO TAKE CHARGE

Before we continue looking at the attributes of effective leaders, I want to take a minute to give you another example of what happens when leadership isn't effective. I want to share this with you now, because we've just finished talking about several qualities of an effective leader that involve interaction with staff and recognizing their strengths and weaknesses so that you (the leader) can make sure they are given the *right* opportunities for *them* in order to reach their full potential.

The Company: BlackBerry

BlackBerry is an example of a great company gone bad because of its lack of effective leadership.

There was a time when BlackBerry was *the* brand to be carrying in your pocket. To do so was pretty much the ultimate status symbol of affluence. So what went wrong? Poor leadership.

BlackBerry was known for promoting within the company—a policy that is usually desirable and respectable. But in this case, it proved to be their downfall because they were more concerned about promoting from within than making sure that those awarded promotions were actually capable of leading the company. They effectively formed the personal connections with their staff, but they used them ineffectively.

Effective leaders know how to handle their personal connections with their staff without putting the business at risk. That's why you need to be aware of the following additional attributes of effective leaders.

Effective Leaders...

- **Diagnose.** Effective leaders have a keen ability to sense what (or who) isn't working and are able to analyze the situation in order to determine what needs to be fixed to improve and/or resolve the problem. They understand the nature of a problem as well as its far-reaching effects. They pinpoint problems through effective questioning and can coordinate a plan of action with staff members when appropriate. After diagnosing a problem, effective leaders also discover ways to minimize, sidestep, or eliminate it.

- **Celebrate.** Without celebrations, work feels too much like *work*, and things that once felt fun can become onerous. Therefore, effective leaders find reasons to celebrate. They keep morale up by ensuring that victories and gains—no matter how small—are recognized in some fashion. Verbal or written, personal or public—celebrations reinforce expectations and serve to propel staff forward. Effective leaders get creative in coming up with ways to celebrate people. This is especially true if there are few or no funds for doing so. For example, they might provide a special parking space, create a monthly award, or pay for a class. But effective leaders also know that the simplest recognition—the words *thank you*—can be the best recognition of all.

- **Communicate.** Communication is the foundation of effective leadership. Without it, leaders stand alone. One of the most common staff complaints we hear is that leaders do not communicate effectively. This may mean that they do not communicate expectations clearly or that they disseminate the information too late, causing people to react to it instead of responding to it by coming up with a plan of action. Effective leaders eliminate confusion by communicating in a timely manner and through a variety of methods (such as email, memos, and displays). By doing so, staff members can all be on the same page. Effective leaders also know that communication is as much about listening as it is talking.
- **Work with Others.** Effective leaders tend to make us feel as though we are working *with* them, not *for* them. They distribute leadership, collaborate with staff, and treat everyone fairly and respectfully. Leaders who work with their staff have a better chance of accomplishing change and creating a stable environment.

Authority is present, but the relationship between staff and leader is collegial, not despotic.

- **Acknowledge Mistakes.** People want to work with someone who is human and fallible, someone who owns their mistakes. Effective leaders are willing to do that. Doing so does not damage their credibility, but actually strengthens it. Leaders who acknowledge errors demonstrate humility and the fact that they are able and willing to grow and learn from their mistakes. Of course, they must also demonstrate their willingness and ability to take action to prevent these mistakes from recurring.

- **Model.** When leaders model the way, they lend credibility to their leadership. As James Kouzes and Barry Posner have noted, effective leaders "take every opportunity to show others by their own example that they're deeply committed to the values and aspirations they espouse. Leading by example is how leaders make visions and values tangible. It's how they provide the *evidence* that they're personally committed."* Effective leaders demonstrate their willingness to benefit the learning community in any way they can, and they never ask staff members to do something they wouldn't do themselves.

- **Commit.** Effective leaders say what they mean and mean what they say. This builds credibility and trust

---

* Kouzes, James and Barry Posner. 2012. *The Leadership Challenge: How to Make Extraordinary Things Happen* (San Francisco: Wiley) among staff members, who realize that their leaders' promises are not empty words. These leaders take on additional responsibilities when necessary; they realize that sometimes they will have to sacrifice their own personal desires and work twice as hard as anyone else to fulfill the vision. They demonstrate patience and fully commit to initiatives—not abandoning them midstream if there aren't immediate results.

- **Adjust.** We've all known leaders who, when faced with adversity or an unexpected obstacle, fail to follow through on the plan of action. "Abort mission!" is their mantra. Effective leaders are able to power through, to regroup and chart a new course. They understand that needs and goals change over time and are able to adapt to meet them. They know that sometimes they need to adjust their leadership style to complete a specific task or when working with a particular staff member.

Last but not least...

- **Lead.** Although this area seems obvious since that's all we've been talking about for the last few pages, it deserves its own honorable mention, so to speak. Effective leaders **initiate** and innovate. They have the courage to make decisions, and **their actions lead people toward the pursued objective.** As former first lady Rosalynn Carter once said, "A leader doesn't just take people where they want to go. A great leader takes people where they don't necessarily want to go but ought to be."

This much I know. I know the power and benefits leadership without management brings to a business. I know because I've worked in both environments.

My first experience (thank goodness) was ideal in every way. The shop's owner was as atypical of the stylist stereotype as you could get. She knew the value of positive and interactive leadership. She knew how to bring out the best in her employees by insisting on a family-like culture. She encouraged each stylist to hone their skills to perfection. She taught each of us how to treat our clients with the perfect balance of professionalism and friendship. She taught us how to be stylists and businesswomen.

But as the saying goes, "All good things must come to an end." So I left the security of home and all the things and people I loved to strike out on my own in the big city— New York City.

This is where I experienced the toxic atmosphere between management and employees in what should have been a "heaven on earth" working environment; I was in a salon on Fifth Avenue—one of the most elite salons in the city—

and I was miserable. The toxicity of the environment was palpable among the staff.

After that, I experienced the stagnancy of a business that saw no need to promote and market their services and the professional excellence of their employees. They were content to stay obscure. The leadership there was basically nonexistent.

My next experience was one with a high-energy and a positive atmosphere that we created. My coworkers and I became like family. The culture was primarily positive, but it was stuck. The shop's owner had no vision for his future or ours.

I, however, had a vision—a vision to take everything I had learned (both good and bad) from the salons I'd worked in and open a salon that gave both the staff and client guests the ultimate professional salon experience.

I know leadership works because I am an effective leader and because I have had an effective leader. In turn, I have helped others become effective leaders—both for their sake and mine.

And now I am ready to help you.

WHERE ARE YOU AT IN YOUR LEADERSHIP SKILLS?

One of the questions I often ask a leader is, "How do you know whether or not you are an effective leader?"

Evaluating your own leadership style, along with your leadership strengths and weaknesses, is crucial to reaching your full potential in terms of effectiveness. In order to help you do that, I want you to take advantage of some of the resources available that will help you do so.

Myers-Briggs tests can be useful tools in determining leadership efficacy. They can help you understand your work and leadership styles, and often offer tangible results that will enable you to work toward self-improvement. However helpful they are, though, these instruments can be cost prohibitive to some.

An alternative and more inexpensive means of self-evaluation is to keep a journal. Simply recording daily interactions and the events leading up to your decisions—and then revisiting them a little later—can provide remarkable objectivity and clarity with regard to your leadership.

The purpose of this type of journaling is to reflect on what you have done in order to better understand what changes (if any) need to be made to make you a more effective leader.

If the thought of journaling scares you or doesn't seem like a good fit, I encourage you to at least set aside a few minutes each day to answer the following questions. Remember, the welfare of your staff, and ultimately your business, is at stake.

Take a recent situation or challenge in your business that presented itself to you, and answer the following questions:

- What *really* happened, or what was the subtext of the situation or conversation?
- Did you identify the desired outcome of the situation before taking action?
- Was the actual outcome the best possible solution?
- What went well? How effective was the method you used in reaching the outcome?
- If it was not effective, what could you have done differently that would have helped you reach a better outcome?
- Are you able to repeat your behaviors that proved effective to ensure similar future outcomes?
- What are you willing to do differently in the future? What *must* you do differently in the future?
- Who were the others involved, and what were their positions, interests, and stakes?

Taking the time to reflect on what took place is a valuable tool for growth and maturity. When we are in the moment, we don't stop to consider what we are thinking, how we are talking, acting, or even leading. But effective leaders find the time to look back on the day's events while simultaneously looking ahead to what they will do in the future.

Set your intention. Before any coaching, meeting, or interaction with your team, make sure *you* know what the intended outcome is. If your intentions are to let them know you are upset, that's all they will get from the encounter. If your intention is that they grow, feel supported, gain clarity, and are encouraged, chances are that will be what they take away.

Remove all judgment. One of the first exercises I do with aspiring leaders is to ask them to send me a daily recap of any staff challenges that they may have encountered. Time and time again, I get reports that say, "Amy is very lazy and doesn't want to work. She hides in the backroom and I have to go get her."

Does this sound familiar? This is an assessment based on opinion—one that will prevent you from properly coaching your teammate. I respond to this by instructing them to tell me the same story without any judgment. An example: "At 11:15 a.m., I found Amy in the back room. I asked her to fold the towels and tidy the staff kitchen. She did what I asked, but I continued to monitor her the rest of the day to support keeping her on task."

Ah, that's better! Now we are working on actually coaching Amy, keeping her on task, and setting a goal for her to learn to self-monitor her workflow.

EFFECTIVE LEADERSHIP

———

Look at these definitions of a manager.

A manager is:

- a person responsible for controlling or administering all or part of a company or similar organization.
- a person who controls the activities, business dealings, and other aspects of the career of another person.

On a scale of 1 to 10, where would you place yourself?

Not at all like me   A little like me   This is me most days   I am the ultimate manager

1   2   3   4   5   6   7   8   9   10

How do you think your employees would rate you on this same scale?

Look at the definitions of a leader. Next to each one, put a number between 1 and 10 to indicate how each one describes your attitude as a boss (1 = not at all, 10 = fits you to a tee).

A leader is a:

- Trailblazer
- Frontrunner
- Organizer
- Chief
- Director
- Guide
- Mentor
- Head
- Adviser
- Supervisor

Who has been the most effective and positive leader in your life? Why would you select this person?

Explain why leadership, instead of management, is a better catalyst for success for your employees and ultimately your business.

Looking back at the traits of an effective leader, what have you done or what are you currently doing to:

- Inspire your employees

- Develop relationships with your employees

- Monitor the climate (or culture) of the workplace

- Nurture—both your employees and the overall dynamics of your business

- Set and maintain the culture of your workplace

- Maintain visibility

Looking back at the two examples of failed leadership, which one of the two examples most closely resembles your business? Do you run the risk of (a) not taking the time to thoroughly train and equip new hires in the culture of the workplace and the business model for your business, or (b) putting the personal side of business ahead of the welfare of the business?

What changes do you need to make to ensure these things don't cause serious problems for your business?

Being visible and present, making a conscious effort to nurture your employees and maintain the desired culture in the workplace are all necessary traits of being a great leader. But along with having what it takes to be a good leader, you need to make sure your leadership is effective. For example, if you are visible and present in your business but don't do anything about what you observe by being there, you aren't living up to your leadership potential. So take a look at each of the following steps necessary to go from being a great leader to being a great and *effective* leader and answer the questions.

A. Diagnose

Are you able to tell who and what is and isn't working? Give an example of when you have done this.

Are you able to analyze a situation to determine what needs to be fixed and how to fix it? Give an example of when and how you have done this.

B. Celebrate

In what ways do you celebrate the accomplishments of your employees and your business?

What do you do to recognize the value of your employees?

Make a list of some things you can do to up your game in terms of celebrating the people who make your business possible. An example: the day off on their birthday, a birthday bonus, or employee of the month recognition (gift card, etc.).

C. Communicate

You cannot expect anyone to do anything if they don't know what is expected of them. What means of communication do you use to convey information to your employees?

How often do you communicate when you wish to make a change to an old standard?

How often do you have one-on-one conversations with your employees?

On a scale of 1 to 10 (1 being not at all, 10 being readily and with ease), how comfortable are your employees with coming to you with concerns and ideas?

What can you do to improve this situation?

What do you do to promote effective communication among employees?

D. Work with Others

How do you express the importance of teamwork and ensure your team values?

Would your employees say they are made to feel like they are working with you or for you? Explain.

E. Acknowledge Mistakes

You are neither perfect nor infallible, and your ideas are not always the best ideas. But then, I'm sure you already knew that, didn't you? The question, however, is whether or not your employees know you know these things.

When have you admitted to your employees that you made a mistake?

How did you rectify the situation?

·

How can admitting your mistakes increase the degree of credibility you have with your employees?

F. Model

Are you ever guilty of modeling the "do as I say, not as I do" philosophy to your employees?

Describe one or two times you have done this.

In what ways do you feel you lead by example?

How aware are you of the various phases of your business operations?

Challenge: Spend a day working with each person or department doing their job. Use the space below and on the following page to record what you learned and some of your other thoughts about your experiences.

G. Commit

How committed are you to making your business a success? Have you demonstrated your commitment by sacrificing your own personal desires, time, and energy above and beyond the norm?

How have you done this?

Do you believe your employees feel they can count on you? If so, in what ways?

H. Adjust

What changes have you led your business through?

Was the outcome positive or negative?

How often do you evaluate the goals you have set for your business?

How often do you evaluate whether or not these goals are being met?

What role do employees play in being a part of the goal-setting process?

Are you willing to listen to their ideas and concerns? Give an example.

Have you ever readjusted a goal or project to incorporate one of their ideas instead of one of your own? If so, why and what happened? If not, why haven't you?

In three sentences or fewer, write out your new or improved mission statement to tell yourself and others what kind of leader you are going to be from this day forward.

YOU CAN COUNT ON ME, COACH!

———

Gettin' good players is easy. Gettin' 'em to play together is the hard part.

—CASEY STENGEL

You just finished learning (or being reminded of) what makes a great leader. But knowing what it takes, and even possessing these skills, isn't enough. Just like a car with a tank full of gas and the key in the ignition has the ability to take you anywhere you want to go, it isn't until you turn the key to *engage* the mechanisms of the engine that the car can actually do anything for you.

So when we talk about what it takes to be a great leader, we cannot stop with the what. We have to engage the what with the why and the how. Otherwise, no one benefits, which includes you and your business.

The how of great leadership can be summed up with the word *coaching*. When we take the coach approach (cheesy, I know, but hey), we send the message that your interest lies in making the business the star of the show, not yourself. In other words, your stylists and any other employees you have know your goal is to **do everything you can to make sure that everyone in the business enjoys the highest level of professional success possible.**

As for the question of why taking the coach approach is so important, I'll let the facts speak for themselves. A recent study showed that organizations with senior leaders who coach effectively improve their business results by an average of 21 percent more than those who never coach.

OK, you say, so coaching is the way to go. Fine. But what's the difference between great leadership and coaching?

TAKING THE COACH APPROACH

When looking at the qualities that distinguish a coach approach to leadership, you need to know that:

- **Coaches take an "ask, don't tell" approach.** Don't tell the employee what to do; instead, ask thought-provoking questions—questions that will require the employee to think. This allows the employee the opportunity to create their own solutions. This is a valuable tool for coaching, because when an employee goes through the thought process to find some kind of resolution, they feel like they have some control over the situation. The solution is their idea. That's a good thing, though, because not only does it assign responsibility to them, but it also means that they feel valued rather than feeling like a scolded child.

- **Coaches focus on the employee rather than the task.** It's about their development as a professional and as an individual.
- **Coaching is not about "fixing" anyone.** Again, it's about their professional and, to some extent, their personal development, and about facilitating the learning process.
- **Coaches set up a clear accountability structure for action and outcomes.** We all need to be held accountable for our actions. Accountability helps keep employees focused on achieving their desired goals. As a leader, it is your job to develop an accountability structure, administer the structure, and *model* the structure. In other words, practice what you preach.
- **Coaching is something that can/should happen as needed and in the moment,** as this is the best moment for learning. It's a great way to reinforce what may have been learned in the classroom by capitalizing on those on-the-job learning experiences.

I am confident everyone clearly sees the value of leading by coaching. How could you not, right? But just as any good coach knows, and just as any team knows, good coaches don't just happen. Good coaches put a great deal of heart and energy into getting to know their players—or in this case, their employees—well. They have to know what each one's strengths and weaknesses are so they know how to best **utilize them instead of using them.**

Getting to know your employees for the purpose of coaching them as effectively as possible requires that you:

- **Ask good questions.** Asking the right questions brings the right solutions, resolutions, and outcomes.
- **Meet the employee where they are at.** We will talk more about this later, but for now, let's just say that as a coach, you need to see an employee for who they are now, in order to guide them toward who they can become.
- **Guide the conversation** (through questions, not directives) toward a mutual agreement on the desired outcome.
- **Ensure that feedback is heard** and understood by the employee. Again, asking clear questions is the best way to do this.
- **Do your part to support the employee** through a shared commitment to their goals and responsibil-

ities, as well as the actions necessary to get them where they want to be.

Coaching = Effective Conversations

Coaching your employees is not a one-way street. Remember, at the core of the coach approach to leadership is the ability to ask good questions; and if you ask a question, you need to be ready to listen to (not just hear) the answer. Conversation isn't meant to be a monologue, but rather a dialogue.

When coaching employees, you need to make sure you are asking questions that are:

- **Open-ended.** Focused on useful outcomes.
- **Nonjudgmental.** Avoid asking why.

Some examples of good open-ended questions and their close-ended equivalents are:

- Open-Ended/Inviting Questions
  - What is the status on x?
  - How can I help you?
  - Can you tell me about that error?
  - Walk me through your thought process.
  - What other approaches might you take next time?

- How are your emotions influencing your perception of the situation?
- Close-Ended/Evaluative Questions
  - Are you finished yet?
  - Do you have a problem?
  - Did you make that mistake?
  - Will this really solve the problem?
  - What made you think that was a good idea?
  - That's clear enough, isn't it?
  - Didn't I go over this already?
  - Why didn't you do x?

Do you see the difference? Of course you do! How could you not?

That just leaves us with one more question—the question of whether or not you are up to the challenge. I hope so, because the success of your employees, your business, and ultimately your career is counting on you. By taking the coach approach to leadership, your employees will be developing and challenged in a way that truly builds new skills, enables them to learn from experiences, and allows them to reach their full potential. And in return, the culture of your business will be the envy of everyone, and you will be enjoying a level of success you never thought possible—financially and otherwise.

WHY SHOULD LEADERS COACH

Managing/leading people in the new millennium is becoming less about command and control, and more about development and empowerment. Increasingly, managers are becoming leaders because they are taking some responsibility for ensuring that their staff members always have the **knowledge** and **skills** necessary to perform at their highest possible level.

When you stop and think about it, coaching is really just a form of employee training and development. But instead of a period of training and development during new hire orientation or a trial period, coaching involves **ongoing training and development**. When new competencies are needed due to a change in the work situation, or when poor performance indicates that remedial instruction is needed, leaders fill the gap and initiate the necessary changes and corrections through coaching.

Leaders should also see coaching as a means to build on employees' knowledge and skills. Unless leaders are handed staff that possess all of the knowledge and skills they will ever need to do their jobs, some degree of learning must take place during the employment relationship. Coaching is simply a way that managers supplement any formal training and on-the-job learning their employees get. It's a means of giving remedial instruction when performance deficiencies necessitate. Over time, coaching can also prepare employees for advancement and additional responsibility.

Coaching can also be part of a long-term effort to promote employee development. One of the criteria on which leaders are evaluated is how well they help others develop into leadership material. A true coach grooms others to someday take their place, to be a part of the coaching team, or even to strike out on their own.

I've heard about CEOs who are highly effective when it comes to expanding the business and boosting stock values, but who do a poor job of preparing their replacements. When they leave the company, it ends up floundering because no one was prepared to take over. This is a classic case of someone who is working *on* their business, not *for* their business. They are, as I mentioned earlier, focused on being the star themselves instead of making the business the star.

COACHING VERSUS COUNSELING

It is easy to recognize the need for coaching when employees have new jobs, duties, or tools, but we often fail to diagnose the need for coaching when employees are performing poorly. In fact, ideally, ongoing coaching should minimize the need for any correction at all.

A recent issue of the *Leader Letter* explains that counseling is the appropriate response when employees' motivation problems are the cause of poor performance, but leaders need to remember that not all performance problems are due to a lack of motivation. Poor performance can also be the result of a misunderstanding of expectations or a lack of skill. Think about it. How many of you can recall a situation when a manager chastised us for screwing something up when all we really needed was a clarification of what was expected? *How demoralizing!*

Although coaching and counseling have different purposes, they *are* related. Sometimes coaching reveals attitude problems, fears, or other *roots of the tree* factors that interfere with someone's willingness to do their job. When barriers such as these are identified as the reason for an employee's lack of motivation, leaders must shift into a counseling mode to resolve the problem before engaging in coaching. Most of us bring our habits and personal histories to work, and that's when the leader has to tend to the roots of the tree, to get the whole thing blossoming. There's no point in working on employees' "can't do" problems before resolving their "won't do" problems.

You also need to be aware of the fact that the need for coaching can also emerge during counseling. For instance, when an employee is intimidated by the complexity of a task, that fear can be manifested in a number of counterproductive work behaviors—one being procrastination. This is clearly a case where coaching the employee toward the level of confidence they need to perform the task is necessary.

THE MECHANICS OF GREAT COACHING

In case you haven't figured it out yet, the purpose of coaching is to provide the ultimate experience in employee training and development for the good of the employee, as well as your business. Whether it's on the job or off, planned or impromptu, coaching works well.

The science of employee training and development can't easily be reduced to a list of bullet point steps to follow, and you may notice some glaring omissions from the list below. But with that disclaimer in mind, I want to share with you what I believe to be the most essential of essentials for taking the coach approach to leadership.

Put the employee at ease. This step is an important first step when coaching sessions take place for a number of different reasons. When the coaching session is the response to poor performance, it is an absolute must for setting the stage for the best possible outcome and resolution.

Find out what they already know. Don't assume. You

hate when people do that to you. There are three reasons you need to find out what an employee already knows. First, it saves time because there is no need to tell them what they already know. Second, it eliminates the chances of unnecessary resentment toward you by the employee. If you tell them something they already know, they are going to resent the fact that you don't recognize their level of achievement. And third, you can use their prior knowledge as a stepping stone for acquiring new knowledge. You can link the training to what they already know and correct any misconceptions that could interfere with their learning.

Present information or demonstrate work methods. This is the point where you deliver the content of the training. You *are* their leader, so lead. Remember, leaders don't just tell people what to do. Leaders show people what to do and ask questions to gain understanding.

Repeat. Repetition enhances understanding and retention. I also want to say at this point that you need to be mindful of how your employee learns best. What is their **learning style**? Are they hands-on learners? By this I mean, do they learn and retain knowledge best when they are allowed to do something while you take them through the process one step at a time? By actually doing something while being instructed on the how-to, hands-on learners get the feel for what is expected of them quicker than they would otherwise. Are they visual learners? Do they learn best when they are given a set of instructions to read or when they watch you or someone else demonstrate a procedure or task? While watching, they are locking the knowledge away in their mind where it will be available for instant recall whenever they need it. Or are they audial learners? Do they learn best when you tell them what to do? Audial learners also like instructions to be placed in front of them, but they will read them (often out loud) in order to make it stick. No matter what learning style your employees have, you need to know that repetition is necessary.

Evaluate learning. Test whether the employee understands the information or can perform the skill. Give them opportunities to prove themselves.

Provide feedback. Let the employee know how their improvement meets or exceeds what you expect of them, as well as the areas in which they are still lacking.

Correct. Repeat the proper methods for doing the task that they are having trouble with.

Evaluate performance on the job. Periodically check to see whether the employee is using the knowledge or skills effectively on the job. Don't take anything for granted. Just because an employee gets something right initially doesn't mean they will forever get it right. Regular evaluations are necessary to ensure optimal performance levels. But after the initial training period, you should be able to gradually increase the time between evaluations because, ultimately, the goal is to coach an employee to the point of accepting responsibility for monitoring their own performance on a daily basis.

Reward. Provide praise or other rewards for successful acquisition and use of the knowledge or skill.

The degree of specificity used in instructing staff members can and should vary. Sometimes the best coaching tool is to guide staff members through the process of figuring things out for themselves. The coach does need to have a system of accountability in place, however, to monitor whether or not the decision reached is the correct decision *and* the best one for the business.

Middle- and upper-level leaders responsible for coaching lower-level leaders and professionals may rely more on monitoring their staff's professional development, helping them see opportunities for self-improvement, and encouraging them to continue to progress in their development. In contrast, coaching entry-level employees might involve much more explicit and regular instruction.

Regardless of what level of coaching is needed, the

mechanics are all pretty much the same and should be applied to every situation to whatever extent is necessary.

MAKING THE RIGHT CALL

Knowing to what extent coaching is necessary with an individual employee requires you to have a connection with that individual, no matter how many individuals you have working for you. To not have that connection would be like standing in front of a display of over-the-counter medications and doing "eeny, meeny, miny, moe" to decide what to give your child when they are sick. My point is, you cannot help someone if you don't know what they need help with.

Over the past few years, as Fox and Jane has been growing and establishing its reputation for being a step ahead of the rest, I've learned a few things. More specifically, I have learned that successfully coaching your employees requires having the right combination of knowing how to coach *and* how *much* to coach.

To help you determine how much coaching an employee needs, I've put together a little outline of **employee levels**. Once you determine what level each of your employees is at, you will be able to know how much coaching they need in order to make it to the next rung of their ladder to success.

LEVEL 1 EMPLOYEE

Any new employee within a thirty-day probationary period.

All new staff, regardless of experience level, should be closely monitored and given specific delegation, including:

- Set up for success by giving instruction before beginning their day and beginning any task.
- Outlined tasks—initially one at a time, working up to a daily list.
- Outlined expectations (be exceptionally clear).
- In-the-moment training—be present and actively involved in what they are doing when they are doing it.
- Constant monitoring and feedback to the team member on their progress.
- Reminders to self-market using social media, Yelp reviews, promotions, and word of mouth.

LEVEL 2 EMPLOYEE

Any employee who is new to a skill or position, but has passed the thirty-day probationary period.

These team members often resist training because they think they know more than they actually know. To prevent this from being the case in your place of business:

- Outlined tasks on a daily basis, eventually transitioning to a weekly basis.
- Regular check-ins—stop by their workstation regularly to say hi, ask if they have any questions, make note of any behaviors that need to be corrected, and compliment their progress.
- In-the-moment coaching, which is hands-on and/or "here, let me help you" coaching.
- Outlined expectations—leaving nothing to chance.
- Course-corrective conversations—private conversations between the two of you for the purpose of taking corrective action now rather than later.
- Consistent monitoring and feedback that is comprised of both praise and tips for improvement and correction.
- Compliment sandwich—the good news/bad news/good news philosophy that works like this: *praise, address the problem, and then praise again.*
- Invite the employee to offer feedback and ask open-ended questions.

LEVEL 3 EMPLOYEE

Any team member who has previous experience in their position with another company, has completed their probationary period, and is within their first year.

This team member should have a clear understanding of:

- Productivity reports—how, what, and why this is required.
- Daily tasks.
- Raises and end-of-year review process.
- Time-off request protocol.

Coaching for these team members should consist of:

- Course corrections—conversations to help redirect a team member who is veering off-course or experiencing a problem in a particular area.
- Productivity reviews and monthly feedback—communicating how well the team member is doing in meeting goals and expectations (including praise, instruction, and correction).
- As-needed coaching based on questions and conversations.
- Monitoring improper behavior and habits.
- Helping to evolve teamwork skills.
- Improving of *business* practices in this employee: use of time, retention of clients, general service skills, upselling, follow-up calls, self-marketing.

LEVEL 4 EMPLOYEE

This team member has been in their position for one or more years.

This team member should have a clear understanding of:

- Productivity reports.
- All standards and expectations.
- Daily tasks.
- Raises and end-of-year review process.
- Time-off request protocol.
- Good relationships with leadership.

Coaching for these team members should consist of:

- Course corrections—conversations to help redirect a wayward team member.
- Productivity reviews and monthly feedback.
- As-needed coaching.
- Monitoring improper behavior and habits.
- Helping to evolve teamwork skills.
- Improving *business* practices in this employee: use of time, retention of clients, general service skills, upselling, follow-up calls, self-marketing.

IMPORTANT

Goal setting is an important part of the process every year. At this point, the team member should be settled in, well trained, and taking pride in helping maintain the culture of the salon. It is important to begin pointing them in the direction of achieving new goals and a higher level of personal successes.

The reason this is so important is because when employees are engaged and enthused about their role in the business, it keeps them in the business—that is, minimal turnover.

Suggestions for Goals to Be Assessed Include:

- Retention of clients (what percentage?)
- Sales
- Product sales
- Mastering new techniques
- Attending advanced education opportunities

LEVEL 5 EMPLOYEE

This team member has been a productive member of your business for two or more years. They hit their goals within the first year and have a clear understanding of company standards and requirements.

This team member should:

- Have a retention goal of 70 percent or higher.
- Can offer support in training of new staff.

- Should be able to clearly echo the values and message of the brand.

The following should be taken into account with regard to coaching these team members:

- Course-corrective conversations should be largely dialogue based, and rarely or never boss-employee based.
- Leadership should ask their opinions regarding goals and assessments of salon life when appropriate.
- They should receive support for the goals they set for themselves, as well as support for following through to meet these goals.
- Inspiration and encouragement to strive for a higher level of professional excellence.

You will rarely (never) micromanage this team member unless they are learning a new skill. If this takes place, it should be made clear to the team member that this is the reason for the increased level of coaching, so as not to demean them or decrease the level of trust and confidence you have in each other. This team member will also be able to clearly communicate with you based on question-and-answer-style coaching.

LEVEL 6 EMPLOYEE: THE FUTURE LEADER

This is a team member who has been with the company for two or more years, *or* during one exceptional year.

This team member stands out as a potential future leader. Why? Because this team member:

- Understands the company values, standards, and mission; and more often than not clearly emulates them.
- Has good relationships with both peers and leaders.
- Has strong base-level communication skills.
- Shows signs of delegation skills.
- Has expressed interest in leadership.

Coaching of these employees is limited to:

- End-of-year reviews.
- As-needed coaching.
- Minimal monitoring for corrective behaviors and habits.
- Conversations regarding assessment for future leadership training.

LEVEL 7 EMPLOYEE: NEW LEADER

This team member has passed a probationary period of leadership assessment and is now in a delegation phase learning a new skill—the skill of leadership.

This team member should focus on:

- Learning all salon processes and accomplishing everything on the Leadership Training checklist.
- Learning to monitor the room.
- Learning to delegate.
- Learning to set tasks and see them through.
- Maintaining personal standards and creating balance in two positions (team member and future leader).

Coaching for this level of employee is a combination of *delegation* and *conversation*.

LEVEL 8 EMPLOYEE: LEADERSHIP

These leaders are generally in their first years of leadership. This phase, however, can last years. Some leaders never pass this point but are still successful and effective leaders.

The employee at this level is learning to balance:

- Staff friendships.
- Boundaries.
- Setting the standards.
- Delegation.
- Assessing employee levels and tactics of coaching.
- Inspiration and motivation (sales vs. praise).

- Goal setting and follow-through for staff.
- Sounding like the brand.
- Team building.
- Respect (given and received).

The level of coaching that leaders at this level receive is usually in the form of the twice-monthly leadership sessions and any as-needed coaching that comes up along the way. As-needed coaching at this level is always conversational.

LEVEL 9 EMPLOYEE: COACH AND MENTORSHIP

This phase is when you begin making long-term personal changes in those around you.

Mentorship is different from leadership. Leader-coaches give feedback and poke holes in someone's thought process. Mentorship helps team members assess areas of weakness for themselves and guides them to create and carry out productive changes on their own. This is generally a long-term, if not lifelong, commitment.

Coaching as a mentor is the ability to teach a skill beyond the boundaries of a given job. Such skills might include:

- Communication.
- Delegation.

- Leadership and coaching skills.
- Handling business issues.
- Breaking down a negative thought process.
- Redirecting gossip, excuses, and self-doubt.
- Teaching teachers.

LEVEL 10: MASTER OF THE UNIVERSE

There's nothing more you can teach this person, and nothing more they can learn.

Let me know if you ever meet this person, because I would like to meet them, too.

IT'S YOUR TURN

YOU CAN COUNT ON ME, COACH!

---

1. In your own words, describe how you think leadership and coaching go hand in hand.

2. Coaching focuses on leading an employee toward finding their own solutions to the problems they face on the job rather than dictating their responses. How does this model work cohesively with the fact that there must be rules in the workplace?

3. Give an example of how coaching an employee toward finding a solution works better than demanding a solution.

4. Would your employees say you care more about them than you do the job, or vice versa? Why would they say this?

5. What does the accountability structure of your business look like? Do you have regular (daily or weekly) interactive sessions or conversations, or are they isolated yearly or quarterly reviews? Explain.

6. How do you think a more consistent accountability structure might help the individual employee as well as the business as a whole?

7. What does the ideal accountability structure look like to you?

8. What needs to be done in your business to implement this structure?

9. In this chapter, you learned what the traits of a good coach are. Let's go back and look at those things. Next to each one, give an example of how this would look in your workplace. Put an asterisk (*) by the ones you are currently doing well. Put an X by the ones you need to work on.

FYI: If you need to, refer to the previous examples listed for each kind of question.

Coaching = Effective Conversations

- **Open-ended questions:** Focused on useful outcomes

- **Nonjudgmental questions** (avoid asking why)

COACHING VERSUS COUNSELING

It is easy to recognize the need for coaching when employees have new jobs, duties, or tools. But we often fail to diagnose the need for coaching when employees are performing poorly. Or better yet, for ongoing coaching to minimize the need for correction.

- Performance issues:

- Attitude issues:

- Lack of motivation (can't do vs. won't do):

Put the employee at ease.

Present information or demonstrate work methods, and repeat.

Evaluate progress and provide feedback.

Evaluate performance and provide feedback.

Rewards.

Take a few minutes to review the ten levels of employees.

Record an example for each using the employee's name, the level they are at, and a few notes as to how you can improve your coaching strategy with that person.

1. _____

2. _____

3. _____

4. _____

5. _____

6. _____

7. _____

8. _____

9. _____

10. _____

11. _____

12. _____

13. _____

14. _____

15. _____

16. _____

17. _____

18. _____

19. _____

20. _____

Coaches in the world of athletics or academia are expected to lead their team toward the goal of excellence by way of their instruction, inspiration, and example. They know the rules of the game and know them well. They know each team member's strengths and weaknesses; using these things to the advantage of the team *and* to build up the individual's confidence and capability levels.

Your business, a.k.a. workplace, is the playing field. Your office is the locker room. Your employees are your team and *you* are the coach. So be one.

RULES VERSUS STANDARDS

———

Rules are expectations...commands, even for behavior—not favors you are asked to do.

—MOMMA D.

As a young woman, I was a rule breaker. In fact, I was downright rebellious. If you were to do an internet search for "quotes about obeying the rules," the results of that search would lead you to page after page of quotes about why it is OK to break the rules, how following the rules stifles one's creativity and individuality, and that the primary purpose of a rule is to break it. I am not the least bit ashamed or embarrassed to say I have tested that theory more than once. What I've come to understand is that the difference between rules and standards has to do with participation: how willing or interested you are to take part. As a young person, rules were dictated to me. Well, that's never quite worked in my case. I'm not sure it's worked so well for many others either. Leadership has taught me that while rules are necessary, standards are the goal. Standards happen because your team wants them to. Rather than forcing excessive rules, your team will take ownership of the standards. Standards come from each person from the ground floor up, and rules come from you.

Of course, rules are necessary for order, organization, and progress. In the absence of rules, you have chaos—and chaos, as we all know, has no business in your business.

While it would be unreasonable to assume there could or even should be a uniform rule book that every business would follow, there are a few basic rules every business needs to have in place and enforce.

THE RULES ABOUT RULES

At Fox and Jane, we have one rule around which all our other rules revolve. **Each member of the Fox and Jane team is expected to be kind, polished, and professional at all times.**

Within the perimeters of these three things, you need to make sure you have rules in place for the following:

- **Appearance standards.** You can call it a dress code if you want, but appearance standards sounds more professional. A code is something they have to comply with, while standards sounds more like a cooperative effort.

Appearance standards also take into consideration the different shapes, sizes, and personalities of your staff, whereas dress codes don't. Dress codes tell people what types of clothing they can and can't wear. Appearance standards take a more personalized approach. So instead of merely stating what types of clothing can be worn, appearance standards focus on dressing in such a way that you present a polished, professional, and poised look.

Appearance standards are meant to help people keep the proper balance of modesty, professionalism, and individuality. In other words, their purpose is to keep you looking your best by being required to dress in such a way that exemplifies your self-confidence and your abilities as a professional. And let's face it, that doesn't look the same for everyone. Your appearance standards also need to be as gender general as possible. The evolution of gender in the workplace has changed, and just as haircuts are no longer gendered, your dress code shouldn't be either.

Setting appearance standards is a necessary rule. If you don't, you are setting yourself up for a culture where employees will consistently try to push the boundaries, play the subjectivity game, and create feelings of resentment among employees.

- **Customer/client relations.** The only thing allowing you to keep your doors open for business is the fact that you have customers or clients who are willing to pay for the goods and services you have to offer. With that in mind, it is important for you to establish rules for your staff regarding how they interact with these people.

I realize that the type of business you have plays a significant role in determining the degree to which your staff interacts with the clients or customers they serve. But to give you an idea of the direction you should take in regard to establishing rules for these relationships, I am going to share with you what Fox and Jane does.

It is the responsibility of your staff to find out what the client wants. In our business, a consultation is where and how this takes place. The consultation is a fact-finding mission. The stylist is responsible for asking questions, making suggestions based on the answers they are given, and repeating back to the client what they've heard to make sure they understand each other. A consultation may take five minutes or forty-five minutes depending on several things, including the prior relationship between the stylist and the client, and the confidence level of the client in knowing what they want.

A customer should not have to provide exact details about what they are looking for or need done. Your staff should know their job and the ins and outs of the business well enough to guide a customer toward complete satisfaction. In other words, a customer should not have to tell your staff what you do or don't have in stock, what your ad says, what claims your website makes, and so forth.

For example, at Fox and Jane, we charge a 50 percent cancellation fee if the cancellation is made less than twenty-four hours prior to the appointment. That 50 percent is, however, applied to their next visit. A client should never have to remind a stylist that they have pre-paid that 50 percent at a rescheduled appointment.

Be good listeners. When you really listen, you don't have to do much guessing in regard to what will bring the client the level of satisfaction they are looking for.

- **Masters of redirection.** Your staff needs to know how to redirect any conversation with a client out of a danger zone to something more neutral.

The areas we encourage our stylists to redirect a conversation away from include religion, politics, gossip, and controversial social issues (beyond the basic, "Isn't what happened to those children in that school awful?"). If you want a healthy team culture, you may also have to redirect your client away from speaking badly about another salon or business. This is your chance to set *the standard* for your customer—we don't do that here. You can use redirection without drawing attention to what you are doing, which might embarrass the customer. They will simply move on with you and know that "Wow! She never let me go down that route." Sadly, a lot of salons *love* to know who in their town isn't doing a great job. To me, this only sheds a bad light back on us.

Likewise, they also need to know how to redirect conversations with fellow staff members out of "no-fly zones" that are counterproductive to maintaining the culture of the workplace. The culture of our salons is to never talk about anything with anyone who cannot help you achieve a solution to the problem. In short, *no gossip or complaining allowed*! If a stylist has a problem with something, they need to go to someone in leadership, because our leaders are the ones who offer solutions that lead to resolution. We like to say, "Talk up if you need help. Talking sideways or down the ladder *is* gossip."

- **Workplace relationships.** While you definitely want a culture that promotes a family-like atmosphere, you also need to make sure it is balanced with professional propriety.

If you are taking the coach approach to leading your business, most of these things take care of themselves. Why? Because when daily coaching is part of the leader's routine, issues are resolved before they have a chance to become actual issues. For example, if stylist A comes to you with the habit of sitting around talking between clients instead of offering assistance to another stylist or taking it upon herself to clean or straighten workstations used by everyone, then a daily coaching exercise asking the stylist what she could have done to make the day better or more productive will solve that problem, *as well as* the potential problems of the other stylists resenting and disliking her because she lacks team spirit.

While I don't claim to have all the answers to creating a healthy family-professional balance, here is what we have found works at Fox and Jane:

- Trust is nonnegotiable. You need to know you can trust everyone you work with, and they need to know they can trust you.
- You have to adhere to the culture of the salon (more on that in a minute).
- Friendships among staff that extend beyond the salon need to be left at the door during work hours. In other

words, what you do away from the salon is your business, but you cannot bring it into the business.

- Leaders/managers need to distance themselves a bit from close friendships with staff members in order to prevent accusations (false or otherwise) of favoritism. My hands-down best friend is also a member of the Fox and Jane team. We don't regularly work in the same salon because *that level* of friendship doesn't work in the workplace. And when we are together, we don't talk about work. We don't allow the two to mix. That's the key—to have the level of maturity to not let the two mix.
- Everyone is coached in the art of redirection. I know I already covered that, but I'm mentioning it again because it really is key to healthy workplace relationships.
- Give one another the benefit of the doubt—always.
- **Deal breakers.** At Fox and Jane, we tell you up front that if you want to work for us, you have to conform to our culture, because our culture is why Fox and Jane is the success that it is. That is why there are some things we just have to say no to, as well as some things for which there are no second chances.

You should have these same policies. If you don't, everything else you do to create a positive culture that thrives on a balance of rules and expectations will be out the window. It can't maintain itself because there will always be someone who tries to see just how far outside the boundaries they can go. When you let that happen without there being any consequences for breaking the rules, others see it as their permission slip to do the same. And when that happens, any rules you have become worthless.

The things we say no to, and that you have to say no to, are the things that disrupt the culture we have set in place. These things include poor technique, a lack of professionalism, and anything that brings toxicity to the culture (gossip, selfishness, arrogance, pushing the boundary lines where other rules are concerned, disrespect, lack of reliability, etc.).

We know our culture is very different from most salons, and a lot of stylists come to us not knowing how to act and thrive in our culture. That is why we teach and coach a stylist toward correcting these behaviors. We even strive to do so, giving them a period of grace to come around to our way of thinking; but if they insist on being uncoachable, they're out.

The same might be true in your case. A new employee might come to you from a situation in which toxicity was the norm. You can coach them out of these habits if they want to be coached out of them. If, however, they refuse to change, they need to go.

The things for which there should be no second chances include:

- Theft
- Lying
- Excessive tardiness
- Maligning the business
- Gross misrepresentations of themselves and their ability
- Blatant disrespect

STANDARDS MAKE GOOD EMPLOYEES GREAT EMPLOYEES

Think back to when you first got your driver's license. In the weeks and months prior to that, you studied the driver's manual in order to make sure you knew the answers to whatever questions might be on the test. You also spent hours practicing your driving skills. You were determined to show them you could merge and change lanes with the best of them.

But what happened after they declared you proficient enough to be granted a license to drive? Did you toss everything you'd learned out the window? Did you drive on whatever side of the road felt right in the moment? Did you stop on red if you had time but blow through the lights if you were in a hurry? Did you ignore speed limits?

Did you make right-hand turns from the left-hand lane? Of course you didn't! You have continued to follow the rules of the road because you know that is the only way to continue to have the privilege of driving.

The same holds true for following the rules in the workplace. These rules are not meant to stifle someone's creativity and reduce them to feeling subservient. Rules in the workplace are for putting perimeters in place that make good employees great, and bad employees former employees.

RULES VERSUS STANDARDS

———

1. What workplace rules do you have?

2. How do these rules fit in with the culture of your workplace? Do they reflect the desired culture? Do they contradict it in any way?

3. What appearance standards do you have? Why?

4. Do you think some of these could be considered open to interpretation in a way that could lower the level of professionalism in the workplace? What are some possible ways you might adjust the appearance standards to make them more of a personalized approach to each person?

5. While excellence is definitely what you should be striving for in customer service, there are times when your employees need and deserve protection from difficult customer situations. What rules do you have in place for this?

6. What are the rules you have in place for assessing the needs of each customer?

7. What changes or adjustments need to be made to enhance the level of professionalism and positive relationships among your employees and your customers?

8. To what extent do you coach your employees in the art of redirection? Give examples of how you do this.

9. How could you improve the art of redirection in your business? How would it change things in the workplace between employees and your customers?

10. What are the *nonnegotiables* (deal breakers) for being employed in your business?

11. How do you convey this information?

12. What are you doing to coach your employees away from these behaviors?

13. In thinking about what you have read regarding rules and the workplace, what, if any, rule changes do you need to make?

CULTURE CRUSHERS

Coming together is a beginning. Keeping together is progress. Working together is success.

—HENRY FORD

Earlier in this book, you learned that workplace culture is the key to a healthy business and that the absence of a positive culture in the workplace is a surefire detonator for implosion. I also gave you a brief explanation of some of the primary elements of a positive work culture as well as a couple of real-life examples of what happens in the absence of any proper culture. Now it is time for us to revisit this whole culture thing—time for us to take a more detailed look at what makes your culture great and what doesn't.

WHAT MAKES A GREAT CULTURE?

Because I prefer hearing the good news first, I want to spend a little time refreshing your memory on what makes the work culture great. Not just good—great.

YOU

The makings of a great work culture start and stop with you—the owner of the business, the CEO, the president, the manager, or whatever you call yourself (or whoever the final authority is). The vibes you give off, the way you treat others, the expectations you put in place, the example you set—*these things* determine your work culture.

Because I am a stylist and salon owner, I'm going to talk about salon culture, but what I have to say is not limited to salons. It applies to any business; so when you read *salon* and *stylist*, or *booth rental space* and *product*, just substitute industry-appropriate words in their place as you read. OK? Good, let's get started.

A majority of the things listed below will automatically fall into place when you **lead** rather than *manage* your employees, using the **coach approach leadership** techniques we've already discussed in detail. I am listing them, though, in order to **make you more aware of the benefits** of coach-style leadership and to **remind you of what you are leading your employees toward.**

A SAFE PLACE TO FAIL

We all make mistakes. You've made your share, and I know for certain I've made mine. But when we create a culture in which mistakes are viewed as learning experiences instead of targets to be shot down with humiliation, accusations, and chastisement, an employee isn't afraid to get up and get back in the game. Wrongs have to be righted and corrective action may need to be taken, but these things *must* be done in such a way that the employee maintains their dignity and isn't made to feel like a *failure*. Remember, failing doesn't make you a failure.

A SENSE OF OWNERSHIP

Employees must be made to feel like they have a vested interest in the business in order for you to be able to expect (and have) their loyalty.

The first chapter of this book was a condensed version of my journey from beauty school to where I am today. It is a story I am thankful for and proud of. The most important part of the story, though, is the beginning. Why? Because if my journey hadn't started with Lenore and the Lemonhead Salon, I have little doubt that my story wouldn't have such an amazing happy-but-not-nearly-over ending. Had my first experience as a stylist been in your (sadly) typical salon where gossip and dysfunction may as well have their own "Open for Business" sign in the window, I would not be here today. But it wasn't, so I am.

Lenore isn't your stereotypical stylist, and she doesn't run the stereotypical salon you see on television, in the movies, or six blocks down the street. Lemonhead is a salon where every stylist feels as if they have a stake in its ownership—because they do. No, they don't actually own any part of the real estate or the entity that is Lemonhead. But they know that their success as a stylist is part of what makes the salon itself successful, and vice versa. The salon needs the stylists, and the stylists need the salon.

We were valued for our abilities and our contributions to the shop's success. We knew that *she* understood the vitality of the shop depended on the quality of the stylists' work, as well as the quality of the stylists themselves, so she treated us accordingly. And because she treated us as quality stylists, that's how we were.

HORIZON LINE

Close your eyes and imagine a beautiful horizon—the distinct line between land and sky. Do you see it? Good.

You can open your eyes now, but I want you to keep the image of that **distinct line** in your mind. This is your horizon line.

The horizon line is the **line** I draw **between expectations and goals** for my employees. Having **this line sets the standards for your business.** The line itself is the bare minimum you expect from your employees. These are the nonnegotiable expectations. Everything under the line is not tolerated.

Examples of horizon line expectations include promptness; ability to professionally execute services; cooperation with other team members; respect for self, clients, and team members; appropriate attire; proper hygiene; and so forth.

Examples of things that fall below the horizon line—things that will not be tolerated—include gossip, tardiness, product waste, undermining teammates, disrespect, foul language, immodesty, and other such things.

Now let's look up. The things you see when you look up beyond the horizon line are the goals you set for your employees. These are the things that cause them to rise above the standard expectations. Continuing education, promotions, rewards, and raises are examples of goals you can set for your employees.

When employees are situated on the horizon line, your culture is healthy and cultivates loyalty and longevity among employees and clients. It also gives them a boost up to reach for the goals you set—making for an even healthier culture and more profitable business.

CULTURE CRUSHERS

Now it's time for the bad news. The bad news is that if you don't protect your culture, it can be crushed to pieces by a few powerful blows. Protecting the culture of your salon (or any other work environment) should really be a team effort, but as the coach of the team, it ultimately falls to you. That is why you have to be ready, willing, and able to crush these culture crushers.

Gossip

Gossip is the number one enemy of a salon. Salons have a collective reputation for it—one that was born decades ago and is still there. The only way to eliminate this culture crusher is to have a *zero tolerance* policy for it. Letting stylists know that gossip is grounds for firing is a powerful deterrent. But don't just say, "No gossip allowed." Instead, model and explain how to converse, resolve conflict, and work together without gossip.

Time Mismanagement

A friend of mine who lives in LA recently shared with me that when she walked in the door of the salon she'd been going to for the last three years, she found her stylist halfway through another person's color. My friend looked at her watch. She was two or three minutes early for her appointment but could see from the amount of hair still needing color applied that she would be waiting a lot longer than that to get her hair cut. She went on to say that the stylist acted as if nothing was wrong. She went right on painting, taking her time, and making no apologies for running behind.

Thirty minutes later, my friend finally sat down in the chair. She likes the stylist as a person, but the delay was throwing her entire schedule off for the day. No, she didn't have anything terribly pressing, but it was the principle of the matter.

When stylists are late for work, don't understand their personal service timing, or don't make efficient use of their time doing a procedure, clients who come in after these mismanagements of time are the ones who suffer. But ultimately, your business will also suffer. As stylists, we know that services do not always run perfectly on time. But we must teach our team that it's the communication where the relationship is made or broken. Giving that same client a conditioning treatment while they waited or simply saying, "I'm very sorry," can make all the difference.

Clients will complain (either to the stylist, to you, or to

their friends). Stylists will become habitual in mismanaging their time, causing even more problems. Finally, this will either have a domino effect on other stylists, *or* the other stylists will complain, causing discord among everyone. Instead, if a stylist is frequently running behind because they are genuinely not as fast as other members of the team, teach them to identify the concern and request to extend their timing. Would you rather give them a few more minutes for each service, or have them rush and receive complaints?

Favoritism

Favoritism breeds contempt—both for you and for the employees suspected of being favored (justifiably or not). Most people have little or no problem accepting the fact that they are not as proficient or experienced as someone else. But they do have a problem when they are made to feel inferior or that they are not as well liked. And quite honestly, who can blame them?

You must treat every employee with the same amount of courtesy and respect. Every employee should know your level of concern and interest in them is the same as it is for their coworkers.

As their leader, it is your job to give every employee an equal amount of attention. For example, when you come in on Friday morning, you can make a point to greet everyone by name, give each person a compliment regarding something about their week, and then make a general inquiry as to everyone's plans for the weekend—**equal attention with no favoritism shown.**

Afterward, or at some other point during the week, you can announce that you would like to recognize certain employees for their accomplishments in meeting goals you set for them or that they set for themselves. **No favoritism shown—just earned recognition.**

By announcing that these people will be recognized and by giving specific reasons for it, you are eliminating any justification for accusations of favoritism.

Remember, goals are those things that sit above the horizon line.

HIRING ROCK STARS VERSUS STABILIZERS

We're going to talk more about how to hire the right people for your work culture in an upcoming chapter, so for now, I'm just going to say that when hiring, every team needs balance. One way to consider this is to evaluate each individual as either a rock star *or* a stabilizer.

ROCK STARS

Highly talented, big personalities, who can be inconsistent. They may be top sellers. Natural leaders. But they are the hardest to coach, and they often challenge you and your authority. These individuals can often become leaders years down the road, after effectively resetting their inclination to be self-motivated. Some will just be top sellers and may always cause you a little difficulty within the team.

These hires are highly valuable if you can do the hard work to train them. I don't recommend a whole team of rock stars if you hope to have a team at all!

STABILIZERS

Slower learners, but once they get it, they will always have it. They are steady, reliable, observant, helpful, consistent, have lower sales, but have more impact on the team environment.

Hiring someone who fits in with the other team members and who won't upset the balance of your culture goes a *very long* way. Stabilizers realize a statement is best made by proving themselves to have a team mentality and that they know the value of working for the good of everybody.

I always try to have a few rock stars and a few stabilizers on every team. Rock stars inspire and break barriers. Stabilizers create consistency and support. Together, this creates a balanced team.

ENCOURAGING COMPETITION AMONG TEAM MEMBERS

Don't allow the culture of your workplace to encourage competition among employees, but rather guide them toward competing against themselves and raising their own bar.

As an example, instead of having a contest to see who can sell the most in new styling products or who gets the most new bookings, let stylists know that everyone who sells more product than they did last month and/or whoever increases their new bookings by 25 percent will earn the privilege of an education opportunity, a gift card, or their favorite morning coffee drink...on you.

See? They don't have to beat anyone but themselves.

LETTING THE CANCER SPREAD

Cancer is one of the scariest words in the English language. It is the word no one wants to hear coming from their doctor's mouth because they know that the word *cancer* is generally synonymous with the words *pain* and *death.* And yes, while there are a few people (usually people well up into their years) who decline treatment for cancer, by and large when a person is diagnosed with this awful disease, they take aggressive action to rid their bodies of it as quickly and completely as possible.

While I am in *no way* minimizing a cancer diagnosis by comparing it to the work culture, it is an accurate analogy. When you have an employee who spreads toxicity—even after being instructed to take corrective measures—you have to get rid of them. Otherwise, their toxicity will spread through your culture like cancer, killing off all the good and bringing pain and destruction to take its place.

Firing someone is never fun or easy, but it is sometimes necessary. These cancers have to be removed for the good of everyone and for the good of your business.

CRUSHES ARE FOR JUNIOR HIGH

You didn't go into business with the intention of failing, did you? Of course not! I know I didn't. I opened the first Fox and Jane (and others since then) because I know I have something to offer and that I offer it better than anyone else. I know that by combining my skills as a stylist and businesswoman with the skills of my business partner and of the stylists we hire that we are able to provide clients with the salon experience of their dreams.

I also know that the experience of our clients is due in large part to the fact that we have in place a culture that gives our stylists the work experience of their dreams.

So don't be afraid to do what I've done—don't allow anyone or anything to crush our culture. Leave the crushing to the kids in school, and get on with making a positive culture the cornerstone of your *successful* business.

CULTURE CRUSHERS

———

In chapter 2, you learned that workplace culture is the key to a healthy business and that the absence of a positive culture in the workplace is a surefire detonator for implosion. This is something neither you nor your employees want. So let's spend a little time making sure you know what to look for and how to make sure culture crushers don't sneak in your door.

The following questions indicate whether or not you are promoting great workplace culture. Next to each one, give yourself (i.e., your business) the grade you think you deserve in each area—A, B, C, D, or Fail.

You: Are you giving off the vibes you want your employees to reflect onto your customers?

A safe place to fail: Do your employees feel safe in making an occasional error and owning up to it? Do they know that failing doesn't make them a failure?

A sense of ownership: Do your employees know how important they are to the success of your business? Do you encourage an atmosphere that promotes a sense of loyalty and pride in the business?

Are your employees striving to be better, or are they happy maintaining the status quo and doing the bare minimum?

Now go back and look at each of these things again. Use the space below to make some notes on how you can improve in each of these areas to ensure your culture doesn't get crushed.

The following are the most common and dangerous culture crushers in a business. Once again, give yourself the grade you feel your business and employees deserve for each of these and make some notes on how you can coach your employees away from these culture crushers.

Gossip:

Mismanagement of time:

Favoritism:

Hiring rock stars instead of stabilizers (people who are self-centered vs. team players):

Encouraging competition among employees:

Letting cancerous culture crushers spread (instead of putting a stop to them):

Remember, the culture of your workplace starts and ends with you.

HIRE TALENT

———

The best leader is the one who has sense enough to pick good men to get what he wants done, and self-restraint enough to keep from meddling with them while they do it.

—THEODORE ROOSEVELT

RECIPE FOR CHOCOLATE CHIP COOKIES

Mix the following ingredients thoroughly:

½ cup sugar
¾ cup brown sugar
1 tsp salt
½ cup melted butter

Add in:

1 egg
1 tsp vanilla

1¼ cup flour

1 tsp baking soda

Chill dough for two to four hours.

Using a cookie dough scoop, scoop dough onto baking sheet covered with parchment paper.

Bake at 350 degrees for twelve to fifteen minutes.

NOTE: Can add nuts if desired.

These chocolate chip cookies are sure to be a hit with everyone. They are the best I've ever eaten.

WHAT'S WRONG?

I want you to take a good look at that recipe. What's wrong with it? I'll give you a minute to figure it out (if you need that long).

The answer is, there's no chocolate in the recipe.

Everything else about the recipe is spot-on. It has the perfect mix of ingredients necessary to produce a soft, chewy, delectable chocolate chip cookie. Everything, that is, except what is needed in order for the cookie to live up to its name.

The same is true for your business. Leadership, coaching, a healthy culture, marketing, location (say it three times)—they are all essential. But without employees who develop and flourish under your leadership, who exude the culture you want to project, and who present themselves and your business in the same light your marketing casts on it...well, if you don't have employees like that, you don't have much of a business. Or if you do now, you won't have it for long.

Over the years, I have learned some valuable lessons about what hiring the right people really means. Some of those lessons have been painful, while others have just been what I would describe as eye-opening. Still others have been either spot-on or pleasant surprises—for example, the stylist that turned out to be even more talented and/or teachable than I could have hoped.

Through my experiences, I have come to realize that it is far better to hire the most coachable person, not the most qualified. I know to some that may sound counterproductive, but once I explain what I mean, I think you will agree with me—or at least appreciate where I'm coming from.

Case in point #1: I hired "Casey" primarily because I felt sorry for her. Her interview started off with "I'm pregnant." *OK,* I thought. At least she's being upfront with me. But after telling me she was pregnant, she then dissolved into a puddle of tears. Her emotional outbreak was really out of proportion to the atmosphere, but I gave her the benefit of the doubt because (a) it has to be scary to be pregnant and unemployed, and (b) it's a well-known fact that pregnancy messes with your hormones like there's no tomorrow.

My gut instinct told me not to hire her, but my heart was pleading with me to give her a shot. So I did.

It didn't take long for me to realize I had made a big mistake. After working for Fox and Jane for only a few days, her leader/manager called me to say that Casey had had an altercation with another team member. She made that same call to me the next week and the next, and the next. She was, quite honestly, a drama queen deluxe. She was unreliable, unpredictable, and brought chaos to the dynamics of her team members.

I tried correcting her behaviors using my usual coaching techniques in order to direct the correction measures back to her. One way I've found to be highly effective for doing this is what I call the WWW + EBI formula. Here's how it works:

WWW (What Went Well) + EBI (Even Better If...) = BFJTM (Better Fox and Jane Team Member)

At the end of a day, I ask the employee what went well during the day, and then I ask what they feel could have made the day even better. In getting them to open up to me, I am able to then share what I believe would have made the situation even better for them and for the salon in general.

In the end, Casey had to go. She just wasn't willing to become a part of the team. I'm not talking about losing her individuality or changing who she was. I'm talking about treating me, her coworkers, her clients, and the entity that is the salon with respect, and to be loyal and trustworthy. I'm also going to tell you she didn't go willingly or easily. One thing she *did* do, though, was to teach me a lesson about hiring from the heart—don't!

Case in point #2: Another time, I moved a team member who was thriving in one position to take on another. This stylist was positive, productive, enthusiastic, hardworking, and talented—a fantastic representative of what Fox and Jane is all about. But when I moved her, things started to change.

She was still all of those things she'd been before, but they didn't show in her work. She simply wasn't a good fit for the position I put her in, even though we both thought she would be.

A lot of bosses would have fired her for being unable to fulfill the responsibilities of her position. Not Fox and Jane. I knew what she was capable of, and I knew who she was as a person. So rather than let her go, she was moved back to where she truly fit, where she was an asset to herself and to Fox and Jane.

Now do you see the difference, and why I have the hiring philosophy I do? It's not so much about what they can do for Fox and Jane as it is about what that person and Fox and Jane can do for each other. In other words, **hiring talent is about hiring the people who are a good fit for the vision you have for your business and who make positive contributions to its growth, while growing themselves as a professional and as a person.**

GREAT DYNAMICS DON'T JUST HAPPEN

Hiring a team that can work together dynamically for the good of the business and each individual doesn't just happen. Good hiring experiences come when you and the person you are potentially hiring have an accurate understanding of each other *prior* to moving forward with a job offer. You need to be as certain as humanly possible that the person is capable and willing to be a valuable and effective member of the team, and they need to know what you expect of them in order for that to happen.

It takes a *lot* of energy, attention, and interaction on your part. It takes coaching and leadership.

It also requires you to:

- Know what you are looking for.
- Know how to look for it.
- Know when you have found it.

WHAT YOU SHOULD BE LOOKING FOR

If someone were to ask you what it is you are looking for in an employee, what would you say? Now, I know some of your answers are going to be job- or career-specific, but overall, here is what you need to be looking for when looking to hire talent—employees who are capable as well as coachable:

- Great attitude—someone who isn't all about "me," who takes the initiative to interact with coworkers and clients, and displays a willingness to work as a team.
- Understands the culture—someone who understands the value of working in the culture you have established in your workplace and respects it.
- No ego—but confidence is great.
- Really wants it—someone who wants to grow as a professional and as a person.
- Isn't overly concerned with what they already know—

someone who is capable and teachable all at the same time.

- Knows the fundamentals (remember, we can teach quickly if strong basics are in place).
- Has a great look—someone presentable, tasteful, and fashion-forward.
- Understands respect—for you, for coworkers, for him- or herself, for clients, and for the business in general.
- Strong *roots of the tree*—someone stable, dependable, reliable.
- Just like a rookie draft—"You came here to become one of us. We didn't bring you here so we could become you."

HOW TO FIND TALENT

- Listen at least as much as you talk during an interview.
- Check references.
- Ask the right questions (including a few scenario-type questions to see how they would handle a variety of situations).
- Don't assume—experience doesn't count for everything.
- Tony Robbins once said that success leaves clues— look for those clues in a person's tone, style, demeanor, posture, eye contact, and so forth. Remember, body language speaks volumes.

EUREKA!

You will know you have found the talent you were looking for when you have an employee who:

- Has stamina—they don't gossip or complain, they take initiative, they pursue professional excellence, and they look for ways to be and do better without waiting to be asked or told.
- Are "tall enough to ride this ride"—loyalty, pride in their workplace and their profession, and they willingly work toward being a team.
- Correctly and maturely handle constructive criticism—no one is perfect and a new hire will always have lots to learn about the culture of the business. Are they up for it?
- They are all for going above and beyond—they don't wait to be told or asked to help, they don't groan or complain about goals, and so forth.
- They readily and easily learn to accept responsibility—not only do they readily own their mistakes, but they are also willing to do what is necessary to be given more responsibility (they are self-motivated).
- They aren't fearful or defensive of being held accountable for their actions.
- They are obviously genuine and sincere with you, coworkers, and clients.
- We recommend a three-step process for hiring—a phone interview (brief), a personal interview (more

extensive), and, in our industry, we do a hands-on interview or demonstration of their abilities. We feel that in taking all three steps, we get to know someone as a person and as a professional better than we could with just a personal interview, which usually indicates more about what kind of impression that person makes.

You also need to make sure that during the interview process, potential team members are made aware of the following:

- The culture of your work environment. Be specific. Don't just say things like, "We all get along here," "We work hard to keep the environment upbeat and friendly," or "Drama and gossip don't have a place here." Tell them what is and isn't tolerated and the consequences of breaking the rules.
- The fact that they will be coached on a regular, if not daily, basis. Again, be specific. Explain in somewhat detailed fashion your beliefs and methods of coaching. Knowing what to expect before being hit with it will go a long way toward making it a positive experience for everyone.

THE VALUE OF VALUES

Every business, regardless if it's small, medium, large,

or jumbo-sized, needs to operate on a foundation of a mission statement and core values. In the absence of these things, a business has no clear direction or route to achieve its full potential. What's even worse is that many businesses that have these things in place still waste time, money, and other valuable resources by not hiring based on their company's values. It's like marrying someone with the intent of changing them. You won't. So remember, **skills can be honed and perfected during on-the-job training. Values, however, cannot. These values have to have at least taken root and already be growing prior to hiring in order for an employee to truly fit into your company's culture in a positive manner.** You also need to keep in mind that **when your company shows evidence of its commitment to its values, the right people to hire will come looking to be hired by you.**

Remember, the dynamics of a workplace filled with employees with these credentials is a win-win for everyone.

You know that. You want that. You just aren't sure it can happen.

Well, I'm here to tell you it can. But I will also tell you it cannot all come from you. You cannot squeeze these things out of your employees. They are either there or they aren't. Your job is to decide if they are. And once you decide that, your job is to guide your team into drawing these things out of themselves and each other by establishing a proper culture and by being a leader-coach with an immovable foundation of expectations and goals for them to live up to and strive for.

There's got to be something in it for them, too.

While it is true that you are the boss (or leader) and that, ultimately, it's your way or the highway, attracting talent to your business requires a few things on your part as well. You have a responsibility to create a desirable culture. The horizon line of expectations and goals you have for your employees should be enticing to them. They should readily be able to see and experience the benefits of these things—of working for you.

As business owners, we know what we expect and want from employees, but what about them? What do they expect from us? This is a question you need to know the answers to *as well as* one you need to address with care and concern. The expectations and goals you set need to be beneficial to them as well as to you and your business. If they aren't, the quality of talent you hire will suffer, and your business right along with it.

So what is it that employees want? When I asked this question, here is what I heard:

- They want to be busy. They don't like feeling as if they are wasting their time or just taking up space. They understand slow times happen, but these moments need to be the exception rather than the rule.
- Respectful environment/salon home. I think we've covered that one pretty thoroughly, don't you?
- To be educated and pushed. They want to be challenged to learn and do more. They want opportunities for continuing education and other programs that will put them in line for advancement.
- A great reputation. People want to work for a company that is reputable in the industry as well as with the general public. They want to be proud of where they work and to feel connected to the values that the company stands behind.

Two questions:

- How well are you doing in regard to hiring talent?
- Are you giving your employees what they need and want?

That last question is a bit unfair because there are always going to be malcontents who will never be happy—no matter what. There are also more than a few people out there who are uncoachable—people who will dig their heels in and refuse to accept coaching that comes in the form of constructive criticism, corrective measures, or team-building tactics in order to mesh into the culture of your business.

When this happens, or appears to be happening, you need to take immediate action.

Every time I chose to ignore my intuition or the red flags that went up during any phase of the interview process, I lived to regret it. I had to work harder to get rid of the unsatisfactory employee and repair the damage they inflicted on the team, and it would have taken considerably less time to find the right person for the team. In almost every case, I broke my own rule and hired someone for the *job* instead of hiring someone for the *team*—someone who could learn or ease into the position. Shame on me.

Don't follow suit. Hire talent, not ego. Hire team members, not one-man teams.

HIRE TALENT

———

What criteria do you use when hiring employees?

What are the definite red flags that turn you away from an applicant?

What would you consider to be your biggest hiring mistake? How did you handle it?

What would you consider to be your greatest hiring success? Why?

How much effort do you put into hiring people who will be a good fit for the rest of the team? Explain.

What is your hiring process? How many interviews do you require? Why do you follow these procedures?

Take another look at the list of preferred criteria for hiring talent. Rank them in order of importance to you from 1 to 10 (1 being the most important).

- Great attitude—someone who isn't all about "me," who takes the initiative to interact with coworkers and clients, and displays a willingness to work as a team.
- Understands the culture—someone who understands the value of working in the culture you have established in your workplace and respects it.
- No ego—but confidence is great.
- Really wants it—someone who wants to grow as a professional and as a person.
- Isn't overly concerned with what they already know—someone who is capable and teachable all at the same time.
- Knows the fundamentals (remember, we can teach quickly if strong basics are in place).

- Has a great look—someone presentable, tasteful, and fashion-forward.
- Understands respect—for you, for coworkers, for him- or herself, for clients, and for the business in general.
- Strong *roots of the tree*—someone stable, dependable, reliable.
- Just like a rookie draft—"You came here to become one of us. We didn't bring you here so we could become you."
- Has stamina—they don't gossip or complain, they take initiative, they pursue professional excellence, and they look for ways to be and do better without waiting to be asked or told.
- Are "tall enough to ride this ride"—loyalty, pride in their workplace and their profession, and they willingly work toward being a team.
- Correctly and maturely handle constructive criticism—no one is perfect and a new hire will always have lots to learn about the culture of the business. Are they up for it?
- They are all for going above and beyond—they don't wait to be told or asked to help, they don't groan or complain about goals, and so forth.
- They readily and easily learn to accept responsibility—not only do they readily own their mistakes, but they are willing to do what is necessary to be given more responsibility (they are self-motivated).

- They aren't fearful or defensive of being held accountable for their actions.

- They are obviously genuine and sincere with you, coworkers, and clients.

How do you reward your employees for their talent, work ethic, and loyalty to the team?

Take a poll among your employees. Ask them what they need and want from their coworkers. How well do these things match up with what you are looking for? What can or will you do to meet their expectations?

What type of training and orientation do you require for new hires regarding the culture of the workplace?

Remember, when your company shows evidence of its commitment to its values, the right people to hire will come looking to be hired by you.

KNOW WHEN TO COACH 'EM AND KNOW WHEN TO LET 'EM GO

One measure of leadership is the caliber of people who choose to follow you.

—DENNIS A. PEER

In the previous chapter, we talked about the importance of hiring talent and how to build your team. Now I want us to spend some time on the subject of coaching your team members through difficult situations *as well as* knowing when to throw in the hair towel (at least in my profession)—how to let someone go and move on.

In order to do that, I want to ask you this question: why is coaching so important in the quest for cultivating your team members?

The answer is that a person cannot learn unless they are being taught, so if you aren't coaching, they can't be cultivated.

My experience has been that when it comes to coaching and cultivating new team members, the number one issue that needs to be addressed is truth.

GUIDING EMPLOYEES TOWARD THE TRUTH

When coaching people, the biggest challenge you will face is helping people accept the truth (mainly the truth about themselves). People say they want honest feedback, but in reality, they don't. As soon as you say something they don't want to hear, the walls go up, and they won't accept it. But it is something you as a coach (boss/leader) have to do. To ignore the truth results in more and more damage being done as time goes on.

Encouraging people to deal with reality and focus on the truth must be done carefully and delicately, yet firmly. It's a tough balance to reach but not impossible. If you push too hard before the person is ready, you will fracture the relationship. If you allow the person to continue operating on false beliefs, their habits only become more deeply ingrained. Either way, no one wins.

SO HOW DO YOU GET THAT BALANCE?

Dealing with the truth goes beyond simple statements such as, "How do you feel about that?" or "Tell me more about that." It involves delving into reality, making discoveries, and finding facts to convince your employee. I recently read a blog about how we sabotage ourselves by arguing with reality. It talked about how attached people get to their stories and how those stories are based very little on fact or reality.

The writer explained that when we don't like the reality we are in, we invent reasons to explain why this reality exists. However, the reasons we invent are actually nothing more than excuses and stories we tell ourselves to rid ourselves of blame and responsibility and place it on someone else. We argue with the truth, he said, because we don't want it to be the truth. We want something else— something to make us feel and look better (in our eyes and in the eyes of others as well). And because we look and feel better by telling these stories, we become very attached to them.

But why do we feel such a need to argue with reality?

Three reasons people become attached or committed to these stories are:

1. They have become "reality." Evidence shows that people seek information that **confirms** their beliefs **and doesn't disprove** them. The deeper your search for evidence, the more you find. In turn, the more evidence you find, the more real your story becomes. To change your entire belief about a situation is a huge undertaking.

2. No one likes to admit to being wrong. It goes against our very nature. But it is also in our nature to overreact, jump to wrong conclusions, misjudge someone or something, and to make mistakes. To avoid having to face the reality of being less than perfect, we create a story (first internally and then externally). Once the story has been created, our level of commitment grows. And once that happens, we don't want to turn back. Sadly, it is only when we are big enough to admit the truth and retell the story truthfully that we are able to move on.

3. It serves them. People can get a lot of attention with their stories—attention they don't want to lose or give up. I have seen firsthand how people use their stories to manipulate others. If this is a habit that people grow attached to, there is usually little incentive for them to deal with the truth.

When you are truly seeking to become your best self, you are more apt to embrace the truth about a situation, no matter how painful. But again, it isn't easy. That's why as a coach, you need to be able to steer people toward truth at a pace they can handle and in a nonthreatening manner.

Accomplishing this will require you to be able to override the four major emotions that cause people to avoid the truth.

HOW TO OVERRIDE DEFEATING EMOTIONS
FEAR

Fear is by far the most powerful motivating factor for why people avoid the truth. People often fear that there is something wrong with them and that the truth will confirm this in other people's minds.

People whose fears are based on these assumptions will make every effort to avoid the truth at nearly all costs. But why?

The reality is that there is something wrong with all of us. When we acknowledge this and even embrace it, it actually helps us to connect to one another on a deeper and more honest level. In turn, we become less fearful because we realize there's not really anything to be afraid of.

Facing and dealing with the truth will make you a stronger, more resilient person. Who wouldn't want that?

LACK OF CONTROL

When other people provide us with the truth and that truth is difficult, it can lead to feelings of helplessness. No one wants to be made to feel that they are not in control of their destiny and their surroundings. When we feel powerless over our situation and surroundings, we (almost) instinctively exhibit behaviors that are defensive in nature. Oftentimes, we do this without even realizing what is taking place.

To help you bring an employee's full talent potential to the surface, you need to be able to convey the truth in such a way that they will feel in control of dealing with it effectively. Taking a "what you don't know can't hurt you" attitude doesn't help anyone. If the employee doesn't know something needs to change, they won't change it. They'll stay stuck in the lie, leaving you with uncorrected behaviors.

LOW SELF-ESTEEM

When people feel broken and defeated, they can't handle being verbally attacked by the truth. People like this either believe they can't change or won't accept a long-term change can be sustained. These people may or may not believe the truth you reveal to them, but they won't change because they don't believe they deserve the good that results.

Truth be told, ego often shows up to act as a defense mechanism. People let their ego loose in order to defend themselves because they don't have a strong enough sense of self-confidence to do that job for themselves. So when we reinforce their positive attributes, instead of emphasizing the ones they are lacking in, we contribute to keeping their ego in check, which is where it belongs.

Everyone deserves to be treated with dignity, kindness, and respect. People suffering from low self-esteem need a good dose of encouragement to go along with that. But this encouragement needs to be sincere and realistic. Otherwise, you will end up doing more harm than good.

NOT WORTH THE EFFORT

"If it's not easy, it's not worth my time" or "I can't, so why bother?" is the mantra of a lot of people who refuse to accept the truth about themselves.

This mindset often accompanies a low self-esteem. It isn't uncommon for people to feel so broken that they don't want to start the journey of self-improvement. The thought of not meeting the expectations they have for themselves or the expectations of others is paralyzing. They would rather stay where they are than risk making themselves feel even worse.

Instead of going down a path that may reveal more skeletons, it is easier to just ignore everything and maintain the status quo. They may not like where they're at, but the hard work involved with change is simply too overwhelming, scary, and painful to take on.

People who reject truth in this fashion believe they are protecting themselves by avoiding the truth; but in most cases, they are actually inflicting more pain on themselves. By believing the stories their mind tells them, they miss opportunities to grow and learn.

YOUR JOB IS TO INSPIRE THE TALENT YOU HIRE

As a leader, it is not your job to make employees successful in their roles. It is your job to inspire employees to self-invest and take control of their own success.

Instead, too often managers end up trying to change or fix an employee. Occasionally, they just throw their hands in the air and terminate someone before they really should.

To make sure this isn't the case in your situation:

- Stay focused on the truth.
- Differentiate between the facts and your emotions in any given situation.

- Share your feelings with a friend, and ask them to keep you focused on the truth.

MAKING THE "UNCOACHABLE EMPLOYEE" CALL

No matter how influential you are as a leader, there are going to be times when you encounter an employee who is uncoachable and unwilling to change their performance level to meet your expectations. The number one reason an employee is labeled uncoachable is their resistance to feedback. This resistance keeps them stuck in behavioral patterns that are a great disservice to everyone involved.

An employee who refuses to hear honest feedback is an uncoachable employee. Even constructive feedback is usually resisted. But constructive feedback is essential to personal and professional development. To forgo giving your employees the privilege of this experience on a regular basis is detrimental to them as well as to your business.

Please keep in mind, however, that just because someone exhibits uncoachable behavior doesn't automatically make them a lost cause. There are times when you can turn a seemingly uncoachable employee around, making them a valued member of your team. But you need to know up front that doing so takes careful maneuvering and some tough conversations.

No matter how tactful and diplomatic you are, there will be times when you feel like you are paddling upstream. Some people simply can't handle honest feedback, leaving you stymied as to how you are supposed to manage these employees. What is the most thorough and effective process for making the call? Do they go? Or do you believe that with some intense and deliberate coaching, they have what it takes to be a member of your team?

Set the tone, time, and place. All three of these have the potential to make a significant impact on the outcome of your conversations and the receptivity of the employee.

Time—it is best to deal with issues right away. If possible, take care of it first thing in the morning. This provides real-time feedback that the employee can correlate back to the event. It also keeps you from stewing or fretting over the situation throughout the day, greatly reducing the chances of upsetting you more than necessary.

Tone—keeping your tone calm and even, even if the employee becomes upset, will go a long way in allowing you to maintain control of the conversation. Having control of the conversation is important because it allows you to better assess the employee's response fairly and realistically. If you don't have control of the conversation, you will be too busy trying to regain control to notice.

Place—choose a quiet place, where you are separated from other employees and clients. A neutral space is typically best—for example, a conference room or open office. The "open" part is important for liability purposes. You would be shocked (or maybe not) if you did your research on small businesses getting sued by employees or former employees. So while no one else needs to hear what the two of you are talking about, it is perfectly OK (and smart) for others to see you talking. On that same note, make sure you document everything. You never know when you might need it again—for both good and not-so-good reasons. And finally, make sure you set aside enough time to have a meaningful conversation, as opposed to a "dump and dash."

Limit your feedback. Don't overload an employee with criticism—even the most constructive kind. Less is always best in these situations. Presenting an employee with a litany of offenses is a surefire way to shut them down before you even get started. If a shutdown occurs, the entire purpose of the meeting has been defeated, leaving no reason to continue. You also need to be aware of the fact that if you are overloading an employee with criticism, you might be the reason they are not responding to you correctly. They may simply be too overwhelmed and feel that sense of hopelessness we just talked about. However, if you give constructive criticism one piece at a time and let them work toward meeting your expectations at a steady pace—one foot in front of the other—they just might end up being one of the best things to ever happen to your business.

Be specific. Provide objective information based on facts. Avoid subjective statements or superlatives ("You always...," "You never..."). When you stick to the facts and have supporting examples, it leaves less room for debate. Facts also make the conversation feel more like a teaching moment than a personal attack.

Be honest with employees. Don't try to soften the blow. When someone is resistant to feedback, the more you sugarcoat the information, the less likely it is they will get the right message. In turn, this greatly decreases your chances of getting the positive response you are looking for. That being said, you need to remember to maintain a positive attitude. Remember to say *and* demonstrate that you want to work things out.

Be clear. Set definitive and reasonable expectations for improvement; make sure they know the changes are to be immediate and permanent. Behavior or performance changes should not be a thirty-day issue. You have every right to expect immediate and sustained improvement, but be flexible in allowing employees to get there. You can do this by establishing prescribed steps, milestones, and markers for improvements. NB: Behavior changes generally take around three months to really take hold, but you should see gradual improvements immediately.

Be honest with yourself. Do not take the time to coach employees if you have no intention of keeping them. If you feel termination is imminent and you are just going through the motions, don't put the employee through the stress of sitting through a series of coaching sessions, wondering if they are going to keep their job or not. If you believe your attempts to change the situation are futile, don't prolong the inevitable.

Let the road go both ways. Allow the employee an opportunity to voice their concerns and ask questions. Their questions, however, should not lead to a debate over your feedback. Whether they see the issue you are addressing as problematic isn't the issue. It is an issue because you say it is—you're the boss. So remember, the conversation isn't about establishing the accuracy of your feedback. Rather, it is about creating an action plan that will bring about change. In the end, they don't have to agree, but they do need to find a way to turn things around, or else they need to turn around and walk out the door.

End on a positive note. Make sure every conversation you have with an employee ends on a positive note. First impressions get things started, but last impressions decide which direction things are going to go. In other words, ending the conversation on a positive note leaves the employee feeling respected. In turn, they will feel a deeper sense of responsibility and desire to make the changes expected of them. In short, they become even more coachable.

Even if you decide to terminate an employee's contract, the conversation should end on a positive note. Wish them well, compliment one positive thing about their abilities, and assure them that you will not deliberately sabotage their efforts to find work (unless there have been serious issues such as theft, harassment, etc.).

A HUNK OF METAL AND A GOLDEN ROSE

I recently saw a social media post from a lady named Joni going through her first Valentine's Day since her husband's death. He'd always gotten her flowers and grape soda (something they had on their first date back in high school). So naturally, she was feeling sad, but then her sixteen-year-old son came through her door. In one hand, he was carrying a long-stemmed rose he had made in welding class at school, carefully painted gold. In the other hand, there was a sack containing a two-liter bottle of grape soda and a bag of his favorite cookies.

"I brought you a flower and grape soda like Dad always

did," he said, "but the cookies are a new tradition—something to make it yours and mine."

Just as that hunk of metal was turned into a priceless (in Joni's heart) golden rose, and just as a little boy can turn into a thoughtful, caring young man, even those employees who seem completely uncoachable will often surprise you. So although it may take time and effort on your part, don't assume you cannot help turn an uncoachable employee into one that embraces feedback until you've done everything in your power to try. Let *them* be the one to decide their fate.

KNOW WHEN TO COACH 'EM AND KNOW WHEN TO LET 'EM GO

The value of hiring the right people for your team cannot be overstated. We aren't perfect, though. You are going to make some hiring mistakes, and there will be times when life gets the better of someone, meaning there are going to be times when you will have to let someone go.

Look at the list of the most common reasons people become uncoachable. What do you think could be done to try to coach these behaviors out of someone?

Fear:

Lack of self-control:

Low self-esteem:

Poor work ethic:

Have you ever had to coach an employee suffering from any of these issues? Now that you have a bit more knowledge on the hows and whys of coaching, what would you do differently?

What do you think about this statement: "It is not your job to make your employees successful. Your job is to inspire them to take control of their own success"?

What are you doing to make this statement true in regard to the way you lead your employees?

At what point do you consider someone to be uncoachable?

What, if any, corrective measures do you attempt before deciding to fire that person?

What is your procedure for firing someone?

If you are putting the time and effort into hiring the right people for your business, you will greatly reduce (if not eliminate) the need for the unpleasant task of firing someone. Why? Because when you know how to hire and take the time to find the best possible people for your team, the need to fire someone won't present itself.

LEADERSHIP TRAINING

Management means helping people to get the best out of themselves, not merely organizing things.

—UNKNOWN

At Fox and Jane, we are all about helping our team members reach their full potential. That might mean becoming a leader/manager, taking continuing education courses, taking on different roles within the salon, or a combination of any or all of the above. We are committed to helping you be the best *you*; that way, the best you helps us be the best us. I *dare* you to say that three times as fast as you can.

That is why we have a leadership training program I am immensely proud of. This leadership program allows our team members to advance in the company; they benefit from the Fox and Jane philosophy on an even greater level.

Our leadership program is also the reason for this book—to give you the tools for training solid leaders to make your business the absolute best it can be. Oh, I know there are countless business models out there that claim to do the same, and I'm not here to discount them in any way whatsoever. But I can tell you this: if you apply the philosophy and methods I have developed out of sheer necessity and based on my experiences (good, bad, and indifferent), I can tell you that you will reap the benefits of:

- A vastly improved work culture
- Less employee turnover
- A team of loyal, dedicated, and highly motivated employees and leader/managers
- A positive reputation among your peers
- A loyal following from clients—so much so that it all but guarantees an increase in income

YOUR ROLE IN LEADING PEOPLE TO LEAD

In order to inspire your staff and produce results, you need to be comfortable with your role as leader. You can't train leaders if you aren't a leader yourself.

Leaders take responsibility by motivating as well as making the tough decisions to take their businesses to the next level. This means it is imperative that you have the ability to find and keep good team members who will complement your skills and assist you in getting things done.

Explaining and understanding the nature of good leadership is probably easier than actually doing it. It all comes back to that old adage, "Easier said than done." The flip side of that coin, however, is that good leadership requires deeply human qualities that go beyond the old-fashioned, conventional notions of what authority and leadership look like.

In today's business culture, good leaders are an **enabling** force. No longer are leaders seen as the kings and queens or the chiefs at the top of a hierarchy, looking down at their underlings from their ivory tower or from inside their glass-encased office. Today's leaders enable their staff to develop and perform at a higher level by coming to them and showing them the way to that higher level. They purposefully and personally align the talents and needs of staff members with the goals of the company.

It has been said that good leadership in today's world is more about **attitudes** than **aptitude**. I think I agree.

THE LEADER WHO SERVES

Leaders have to serve in order to truly be leading. This service-based leadership:

- Works alongside staff instead of merely overseeing work being done.
- Encourages.
- Knows the *person*, not just the staff member.
- Values other opinions.
- Bears the weight of responsibility but shares the benefits of success.
- Leads the way for the purpose of preparing others to do so.
- Isn't threatened by the success and capability of staff members.
- Does for the good of all, not for the good of one.

Of course, leadership involves decisions and actions relating to all sorts of things related to being in charge, but a leader's primary concern should always be for the people, because without the people, the business ceases to exist.

NOT THE SAME THING

Leadership and management are commonly seen as the same thing. They are not. Back in the chapter "Effective Leadership," we looked at the difference between the two. Take a look at the terms used to describe a leader:

- Trailblazer
- Frontrunner
- Organizer
- Chief
- Director
- Guide
- Mentor
- Head
- Adviser
- Supervisor

When you look at the qualities of a leader listed above, it should be obvious that what I said earlier is true—leadership at its best is about character (behavior) first and skills second. You cannot look at this list and miss the fact that leadership equals involvement—involvement that requires more than issuing memos and directives.

As a leader, it is your responsibility to *guide* and *mentor* your leaders-in-training toward being this person to the team they are entrusted with. By coaching them to effectively use the leadership approaches we are about to look at, they *will be* trailblazers, frontrunners, organizers, chiefs, directors, guides, mentors, heads, advisers, and supervisors who are respected, admired, follow-worthy, and a business asset you won't find in any stock option.

APPROACHING LEADERSHIP FROM THE SUCCESS ANGLE

Not long after opening the Fox and Jane door for the first time, I came to realize that I cannot be everywhere at once. Neither can I be all things to all team members. To try would have been:

- Detrimental to my health.
- A surefire way to implode the salon before it even had a chance to take off.
- Placing unfair and unrealistic expectations on myself.
- Unfair to my staff by neglecting to fully meet their needs.
- Unfair to my staff by not allowing them the opportunity to grow in their profession.
- Unfair to Fox and Jane by not operating and leading it toward its full potential.

Ask any small business owner what their biggest issues are in regard to running their business, and most will tell you something to the effect that they are exhausted. They are tired of having to do everything themselves and knowing things will fall apart if they aren't there. At the very least, they will probably feel there are many things that won't or can't get done unless they do them.

In my opinion, anybody who finds themselves in that situation has chosen to be there. They have chosen to keep a tight grip on things instead of investing in their staff by training them to become more invested in the business and becoming more a part of the business. Leadership training isn't just about making sure you have someone who can cover things while you are away. Leadership training is about equipping outstanding members of your staff to be you in your absence.

Our leadership training model is all about coaching our leaders-in-training to embody the character traits of a leader even more than they already do. FYI, if they didn't already have those traits to some extent, they wouldn't have been selected to be a leader-in-training.

Are you ready to discover how you can make this happen? Then let's get started.

THE *D* WORD

Delegation. Delegation is to leadership training what location is to real estate. If you want someone to lead, you have to give them something to do. Wearing the title of leader but not being allowed to lead is frustrating. Your wards will feel cheated, disrespected, and underappreciated. And guess what? It doesn't work out so well for you either. By teaching your leaders-in-training how to lead, you are *delegating responsibilities over to them so that you can focus* on the overall success of your business by taking care of "boss stuff" and actively coaching all staff members in a more personalized manner. Delegation saves you time, develops your people, grooms a successor, and motivates everyone to do their best.

Delegation is the means by which we grow in our job. Delegation enables one to gain experience in order to move forward and take on even more and greater responsibilities. Like anything else, however, there is a right and a wrong way to delegate responsibilities. As a delegator, you must ensure delegation happens properly.

TEACHING THE FUNDAMENTALS OF DELEGATION DONE RIGHT

SELECT THE INDIVIDUAL OR TEAM

Who are your potential leaders? Or maybe the bigger question is, how do you *decide* who your potential leaders are?

Potential leaders are those who willingly take on more without being instructed to or asked. They are the people who:

- See something that needs to be done, so they do it.
- Offer to help a team member who is in need of an extra set of hands, falling behind, or in need of encouragement and/or instruction.

- Make new team members feel welcome and valued.
- Make suggestions for improving the work culture, organizational issues, and efficiency.
- Have a positive attitude and an interest in advancing their professional skills.
- Are confident without being egotistical.
- Show respect for everyone and for the business itself.

These are the people you know you can trust. These are the people you want working for and with you for years to come.

DEFINE THE TASK

The next step in training a leader is to define what it is you want them to do. This might sound silly or like an overstatement of the obvious, but it's not. You might be surprised to know how many business owners fail to provide their managers (leaders) with a clear job description.

"Carly" had worked in a boutique for three years, and she was excited about being named manager for a boutique's new location. She was offered the promotion during her last semester in college. Because her degree was in marketing, she assumed she would be able to use her skills to help take the boutique to the next level while building the clientele at the new location. Her expectations were somewhat justified. Her boss had previously put her in charge of three different marketing campaigns. What's more, she had also been managing the surveys used to decide where the boutique's new location should be.

But when Carly went to her boss with a marketing strategy for the new store, she was shot down. And when her boss came in and found that Carly had rearranged the boutique's merchandising layout, she chastised Carly for overstepping her authority.

Carly was both hurt and frustrated, so she asked her boss what exactly she was allowed to do as the manager of the boutique. The answer she got was that her new role was more restricted than what she'd previously done as just an employee. Carly expressed her disappointment and confusion; she felt she had earned more respect and trust than was being demonstrated.

Carly had no trouble finding another job—one where she would be delegated responsibilities she was capable of handling with ease. When she handed in her two weeks' notice, her boss couldn't understand why she was leaving. She couldn't understand why Carly felt she should be able to take such an active role in *her* (the boss's) business.

"I love the store. I just wanted to use my skills to help it grow. I also thought you trusted me enough to know that's what I was doing and that the work I'd already done was proof of my ability to do so."

Make no mistake about it—there will be moments when new leaders let their new responsibilities go to their head. They fall into the old-fashioned mindset that leading is about being on top and looking down instead of being at the bottom and giving team members a leg up. It even happens to the best of leaders from time to time. But by making sure you clearly define the tasks team members are to carry out *as well as* those they aren't, ego won't be able to interfere as easily or as often as it otherwise would.

Defining the tasks to be carried out by your leadership team happens through:

- Regular coaching as already defined and outlined in this book.
- Job descriptions and expectations that are clearly stated.
- Regular leadership training sessions to discuss any new questions or issues, and to allow leaders to express concerns, make suggestions, and so forth.

AWARENESS TRAINING

Leaders-in-training need to be trained how to:

- Spot opportunities to delegate.
- Select the right person to delegate to.

This is essentially training future leaders to do what you are doing—relinquish their hold on things, allowing the team they are leading to be active participants in the business beyond their required duties. For example, salon products available for sale need to be dusted and rearranged on a regular basis, otherwise the products will look old and untouched. This task is not something a leader should spend time doing, but it *is* something a leader should delegate to someone else in order to make sure it gets done. This is "spotting an opportunity to delegate." A leader should look around the workplace for someone who is in between clients, waiting for a color or perm to time out, or someone who is experiencing downtime for any number of reasons. The leader should then select that person to delegate the responsibility to.

How do you "awareness train"? By delegating potential leaders to do these things for you, that's how. When you delegate responsibilities to them, you are coaching them toward developing a sense of awareness of the things that need to be done. You are also giving them a sense of ownership of the business beyond their prescribed duties and responsibilities, and allowing them to exhibit other skills and talents. These skills and talents might be anything from an eye for merchandising and organizational skills to techniques that showcase their level of professionalism, but doing so is a giant step in the right direction for both of you.

EXPLAIN YOUR REASONING

Have you ever been given a task and felt certain it was just to keep you busy or was an unnecessary routine? Yikes! It's incredibly frustrating and demeaning, isn't it? Or do you remember when you asked your parents, "Why?" and they replied, "Because I said so"? Hearing the word *because* come out of their mouths made you feel like giving up instantly, didn't it? Go ahead, be honest.

Guess what? The same thing happens in the workplace when you don't provide reasons for delegating the task *and* why you are doing it in the first place. To help you see this point, let's go back to the example of cleaning and arranging salon products offered for sale.

Delegating the task of cleaning and rearranging these products should be accompanied by an explanation of the reasons for doing so. Telling a stylist experiencing downtime to clean and rearrange the product without any explanation will do nothing more than make them feel like they are being punished for not having their chair full every minute of the day. They might also feel that you are picking on them or that you don't like them. Their reasoning might be if you liked them, you wouldn't make them do something so menial and senseless.

Now let's add an explanation to the delegation:

"Lucy, since you are in between clients right now, I need you to dust and rearrange the products on the shelf in the welcome area. I'm going to announce an incentive reward contest later this week that will allow you all to earn commission based on the amount of product you sell. The packaging seems to be one big dust magnet, but if we make it look as appealing as possible, you will all have an easier time selling it."

See what a huge difference that makes?

REQUIRED RESULTS

What are the desired end results of the task(s) you are delegating?

Not only do would-be leaders deserve to know what is expected of them and why, but they also deserve to know *what* you want them to achieve. Ensuring this takes place rests solely on your shoulders. Nobody can read your mind. They shouldn't have to.

Parents of toddlers don't just tell their little ones not to touch the stove. They tell them *why* they shouldn't touch the stove. "Don't touch! It's hot!" Show your would-be leaders this same degree of concern and consideration for their success.

When relaying this information to your leaders, it is imperative that you take the time to make sure they understand what is being told to them. This is best done by asking them to repeat back to you what you've said. Let's look at an example.

Me: "I need you to be my eyes and ears today in regard to Tessa's work. We've received two calls from her clients saying they were dissatisfied with the way she cut their hair. Both are clients she's had for over a year, and both said they felt like her mind was someplace else. So I need you to observe how she interacts with her clients today, and if you get the chance, just casually visit with her to see if you pick up on those vibes."

Leader: "OK, I'll be glad to."

Me: "I'll talk to her about the phone calls when I do her weekly coaching, so don't say anything about them. And unless she admits she's off her game, don't suggest that she is. Are we on the same page as to what I need from you?"

Leader: Repeats what you've asked her to do to ensure she understands.

NB: She repeats what you've asked of her because you have coached her to do so.

CLARIFY AVAILABLE RESOURCES

Lewis and Clark were commissioned to explore the western territory without knowing where they would ultimately end up or what they would encounter along the way. However, they did not leave on their expedition without spending a fair amount of time being schooled in the areas of botany for purposes of using plants for medicinal and eating purposes, celestial navigation methods, medical treatment practices (sutures, wound care, etc.), and other such things that might prove to make the difference between life and death.

"Great history lesson," you say, "but what does that have to do with training leaders to help me run a successful business operation?" Answer: quite a bit.

While it is safe to say western expansion isn't on your business agenda, there are certain resources necessary to do just about any task. As a business owner, it is your responsibility to make sure the people you choose to help you lead your business have access to the resources necessary for them to adequately complete the tasks delegated to them.

Don't assume they know what these things are or that they know you have granted them access to them. When delegating a task, make sure your leaders understand what resources they are to use. Resources can include people, equipment, money, and even time. So in addition to letting your leaders know what they have access to, you need to make sure they know how to use their resources properly and to what extent they can be used.

DEADLINES

When must the job be finished? Or, if an ongoing duty, how often will they be reviewed? When are the reports due? And if the task is complex and has parts or stages, what are the priorities?

At this point, you may need to confirm understanding with the other person of the previous points, getting ideas and interpretation. As well as providing you with proof that they are up to the task, this step also serves to reaffirm the leader's commitment to their role as a leader.

SUPPORT AND COMMUNICATE

More often than not, your leaders aren't the only ones

who need to know what is expected of them, why and how the job is to be done, and what the expected outcomes are. In order for a leader to effectively lead, their team needs to know whom to look to. As the "buck stops here" person, you need to work with your leaders to convey this message to their peers and teammates. Don't leave a new leader to inform the rest of the team of their new responsibilities. This is something the two of you need to do together.

By showing support for your leaders and working with them to communicate new leadership, big changes in policy, or other major announcements, you are showing your entire staff that team leaders are acting and speaking on behalf of you and the business.

Exhibiting this type of support also serves to reduce in-house drama, resentment, resistance to compliance, and accusations of ego antics on the part of the leader.

FEEDBACK

Whether you are training or sustaining leaders in your business, feedback is an essential part of the process. Remember, leadership training is a form of coaching, and coaching always includes constructive feedback.

You cannot expect someone to change their performance

practices if they aren't made aware of the need for them to do so. Neither can you expect them to be assertive and confident if they aren't given the courtesy of being commended for the great job they are doing. Feedback provides direction to everyone from the newest kid on the block to the highest level of management. Direction determines where we end up. So when you put the two together, here is what you get:

Feedback + Direction = Optimal performance and attainment of goals

LEADERSHIP TRAINING

———

1. Which of the following benefits is most appealing to you? Each one is a result of training up *leaders* rather than *managers*.
   A. A vastly improved work culture.
   B. Little or *no* staff turnover.
   C. A team of loyal, dedicated, and highly motivated employees and leader/managers.
   D. A positive reputation among your peers.
   E. A loyal following from clients—so much so that it all but guarantees an increase in income.

Why?

2. Now look at the benefits again. How would each of them improve a specific problem or issue in your business?

   A. A vastly improved work culture.
   B. Little or *no* staff turnover.
   C. A team of loyal, dedicated, and highly motivated employees and leader/managers.
   D. A positive reputation among your peers.
   E. A loyal following from clients—so much so that it all but guarantees an increase in income.

3. Who does your leadership team consist of currently?

4. How well do you think this is working for you and your business? Explain.

5. What grade (A, B, C, D, or Fail) would you give yourself for the task of delegating?

6. Who on your staff displays the following leadership characteristics?

    A. Sees something that needs to be done, so they do it.
    B. Offers to help a team member who is in need of an extra set of hands, running behind, or in need of encouragement and/or instruction.
    C. Makes new team members feel welcome and valued.
    D. Makes suggestions for improving the work culture, organizational issues, and efficiency.
    E. Has a positive attitude and an interest in advancing their professional skills.
    F. Is confident without being egotistical.
    G. Shows respect for everyone and for the business itself.

7. What opportunities are you giving them to grow their leadership potential?

8. How would training potential leaders enhance your role in your business?

9. Look back at the grade you gave yourself as a delegator. What would you need to do to bring that grade up to an A? Try to be specific.

10. If you have trouble delegating responsibilities in the workplace, what do you believe is the reason for this?

11. How would you describe your feedback delivery? What changes do you need to make so that your delivery will encourage potential leaders to rise to their potential?

12. Do you offer opportunities to rise through the ranks to positions of leadership? If so, what are the rewards? If not, why don't you?

13. You've learned about how to train leaders to help lead your business and how important this is. What changes are you going to make as a result? Use this page to write down some ideas on who you believe is worthy of making a leadership investment in, as well as some specifics on what your process will look like and the outcome of this training.

You cannot be all things to all people, and you cannot be everywhere at once. You need a few people you can count on to keep your business running in your absence and/or alongside you. Don't cheat yourself or your business out of the benefits of doing so.

THE BUSINESS OF BEING IN BUSINESS

———

A leader leads by example, whether he intends to or not.

—UNKNOWN

At the risk of sounding corny, though I hardly care if I do, I'm going to say this: **my business—Fox and Jane—is my spiritual journey.** It is where I learn, where I dig deep into myself to see what I'm made of, where I set goals, where I achieve goals, and it is responsible for helping me to become my best self. My Fox and Jane journey has empowered me to be a more thoughtful and giving person. It has taught me the value of communication, evaluating and assessing situations before jumping to conclusions, and it has shown me the power of what leading others to lead—not just follow—can achieve.

THE BUSINESS OF OWNING A BUSINESS

Being an effective leader—one who leads by example—is paramount to the success of your business. But we both know there is more to running a business than creating the right culture, hiring the right people, and leading them effectively. When you own a business, there is business *you* have to take care of. Things such as marketing, taxes, permits, profit and loss reports, projections, and a host of other such matters have to be dealt with on a regular basis.

Letting these things slide or not doing them proficiently and efficiently will eventually start gnawing away at the quality of the product or service you are offering. For example, the "Vintage Image," a small salon in the Midwest, was doing a great job as far as creating a positive culture in their shop, and Lily was on the ball when it came to coaching her team. She was also enjoying the fact that the salon was making good money. But Lily hated the paperwork that went with owning her own business. She put everything off until the last minute and then begged her family and friends for help.

It wasn't until she ran a small ad campaign and didn't proofread the text that she finally decided to get her act together. Instead of reading "Half Off All Salon Products with Haircut," it read, "Half Off All Salon Products and Haircuts." She pulled the ad off the salon's social media, but not before the ad had been shared dozens of times. Lily lost several hundred dollars that day because of negligence and a lack of attention to detail.

Another example of this behavior could be seen in the salon that my friend Billy and I went to San Diego to rescue. In this instance, the owner's lack of priorities is what led to her business's demise. She was more concerned about being recognized for her own professional skills than about having a salon that offered quality professional services and skills.

When we came on the scene and started initiating the business principles—that is, culture, coaching, and so forth, which Fox and Jane was thriving on—she wouldn't conform. She wanted the shop fixed, but she didn't want to change anything about herself to make that happen.

When it was all said and done, she left because she wasn't willing to make the necessary changes in her attitude and approach to business. She wanted the business to revolve around her and no one else, and it just doesn't work like that.

HOW TO BE ALL ABOUT THE BUSINESS WITHOUT THE BUSINESS BEING ALL ABOUT YOU

For the next few minutes, we are going to look at the more

technical side of running a business. I know—it's not all that fun (to most people anyway), but it has to be done. It just has to be.

#1: Know *the* business. Having investors is one thing, but unless they are well-versed or trained in the specifics of your particular business, they need to be silent investors (for the most part, at least). Think about it. You wouldn't want to send your child to a daycare facility owned by someone who didn't like children, would you? Hint: Matilda and Trunchbull. Neither would you trust:

- A stylist who graduated from the school of culinary arts.
- A financial advisor who can't tell you what a bull market is.
- A mechanic who can't tell you whether or not your battery is charged.
- A doctor who is obese and smells of cigarette smoke.

Or what about the business that is stuck in the nineties, doing things the way they've always been done and refusing to see that modifications need to be made to adapt to the needs and wants of their customers?

I saw firsthand how a lack of knowledge about the beauty and salon industry proved to be detrimental to one of the shops I worked in after arriving in New York. Their obvious lack of concern for what men and women were looking for in a salon experience showed in every nook and cranny of the room. The owner was fortunate in the fact that somehow or other he had managed to hire stylists (including me) with a passion for their profession and who made each client look and feel amazing. He did not have a successful business. He had stylists who strived for success on a personal level.

Knowing the business or industry you are in is imperative, because if you don't, you will have zero credibility. If you don't have credibility, you won't have people's trust. Without people's trust, you won't have a client base. And without clients, you won't have a business.

#2: Know *your* business. How many times have you read or heard about a business going broke because a trusted associate has been embezzling for two, three, or even five years? Or how about the business that is rocked when office romances or other hotbeds of drama are exposed, causing chaos and turmoil?

If you are not personally touching base with management and making yourself aware of what is being done, how it is being done, and the effects of what is taking place, you are going to end up in trouble. I'm not saying you have to be a control freak or that you cannot or should not delegate responsibilities, because you most certainly shouldn't be a control freak and you most certainly should delegate responsibilities. But as I mentioned earlier, you are the person with whom the buck stops. Someone has to be the endcap of authority, and you are that person.

Another aspect of knowing *your* business is knowing your staff's strengths and weaknesses. We talked at length about this in the chapter on hiring, but it was more about hiring people who are good fits for your business. What I'm talking about here is being aware of what happens after they are hired.

- Are they consistent in their performance?
- Are they more proficient in some aspects of their job than others?
- Does your staff feel safe enough to come to you if a personal crisis arises to discuss how to best deal with the situation without it negatively affecting their good standing in the business?
- When you make decisions about promotions, are you doing so based on what you *know* from observing and interacting with the candidates and monitoring their data? Or are you basing your decisions on hearsay and faceless applications and résumés?

The better you know your business, the better off your business will be.

#3: Your network is like oxygen. Small businesses cannot do everything in-house that a business needs to do in order to be successful. We are too busy doing our thing to have the time and energy to figure some of these things out. For example, we all know the importance of having a strong online presence—one that is easily found and easily navigated. It is unreasonable to expect most small businesses to have a tech guru on staff who can keep your site looking dynamic and up to date and to monitor its stats (number of hits, search engine optimization, comments, etc.). In most cases, it wouldn't pay for you to have an IT person on the payroll full time or even part time to do these things. Am I right?

That's where having a network comes into play. Just as you have your area of expertise, there are freelancers and small businesses out there who will do that for you. They will build and maintain your website, your online store, your business's social media pages, and all those other things that give you the strong online presence a business needs these days.

Because they are contracting their services out to you, you pay for only the projects you hire them for or a set fee for scheduled services. You don't pay benefits, payroll taxes, or a regular salary.

This is just one example of how your network can work

for you. We'll look at a few more in just a minute, but for now, what I want you to understand is that networking can make your business stronger, more successful, and save both money and stress. That's a win-win in my book.

I strongly suggest, however, that you look beyond your circle of family and friends to establish this network of business associates. Depending on your husband, your sister-in-law, your best friend's boyfriend, or your neighbor can cause unnecessary trouble and be the ruination of an otherwise solid relationship between you and someone you care about.

This is not to say you should never hire a friend or family member, but the fact that you have a prior relationship should *never be the reason* you hire them. To hire someone for any reason other than their capability to do the job effectively, efficiently, and economically is a poor business decision on your part.

If you do choose to do so, you should never assume you have an understanding of the terms of the project. Your expectations for work being done—which includes time lines, budget, available resources, objectives, and so forth—should all be clearly outlined and agreed upon prior to working together. Having a contract for services in place is *not* an indication of your distrust or uncertainty in the person's capabilities. It is just good business, so please don't let anyone convince you otherwise.

Another reason why I am against depending on family and friends is the fact that doing so severely limits your options. Using freelance sites such as Upwork and LinkedIn broaden your potential for hiring top-notch talent. Both of these sites, as well as a few others, allow you to find qualified professionals you would never meet otherwise. And because they are freelancers, they have fewer overhead costs, so they are usually more cost-effective for you.

Another great source for freelance work is the college or university in your area. Upperclassmen and grad students are always looking for internships and businesses they can partner with to complete projects necessary for graduation. The upside of this is that their work is monitored and graded, so you know they're going to give it their best effort. It is also very cost-effective. The downside to using students is that you'll get to use them only once because when they complete the internship or project, they move on. So in the event you hire someone you really like who does a really great job for you, chances are they won't be available for the next project—unless, of course, they decide to freelance.

Whether you work with someone online or simply hire

local freelancers, having a network of reliable, trustworthy, and qualified people to call on is definitely something worth considering for a number of things, including:

- Website development and maintenance.
- App development and management.
- Software development and management.
- Marketing and advertising campaigns.
- Database administration.
- Graphic design (logos, product labels, branding, photography).
- Copywriting.
- Technical writing.
- Demographic research and surveys.
- Customer service calls.
- Email campaigns.
- Social media management.

The last thing I want to say about the advantages of having a business network is that you build relationships among your peers—relationships that often translate into helping each other's businesses to grow. Here are a few examples of what I'm talking about.

- Dina owned a midsize greenhouse where she raised bedding plants and unique houseplants to sell on site and at local farmers' markets. She usually ordered most of her seeds from a seed catalog put out by a company for commercial growers. But when she discovered a local farm/feed store carried most of what she needed, she talked to them about ordering for her earlier in the year so she would have the bedding plants ready for spring sales. Because they appreciated her business, they agreed to sell her bedding plants instead of purchasing from a supplier from out of town. Both businesses increased their income and formed a business alliance.

- Tressie and Sloan hired a network of college students to help them when they opened up their fancy breads and gift shop. The students' word-of-mouth publicity brought in lots of other students as well as their parents when they came for parents' weekend and sporting events. One of those parents just happened to be a state legislator. Another just happened to be the owner of a high-end café in a major city. The state legislator has now been ordering Christmas gift baskets from Tressie and Sloan for her employees and constituents for the last six years and has no intention of discontinuing the practice. The owner of the café now uses Tressie and Sloan's breads as well as two bread spreads Sloan created exclusively for the café.

- The president of a small-town bank volunteered the bank's large meeting room and his time to serve dinner at a benefit meal and auction for a little boy in the community who was terminally ill. The regional director for the children's cancer foundation was so impressed by this man's generosity and caring attitude that he switched his account to the local bank, along with several other local people and regional businesses.

- Tim hired his former college roommate, Jason, on a freelance basis to design the website and generate an online presence for his new real estate business. Three years later, the roommate inherited a piece of real estate on which he decided to develop a mini-community for senior citizens. The little community would have small single dwellings, a small apartment building, a gathering center with a large kitchen and dining area, a recreation room and gym, indoor and outdoor pools, a small grocery store, gas station, café, and a few other businesses. Because Tim used his services on a somewhat regular basis, Jason decided to give Tim first dibs on selling the lots and managing the apartments and retail spaces. Both Tim and Jason prospered because they had a network relationship.

Creating a network is about making connections. Connections create stability, which is at the top of every business's list of priorities. So get out there and start connecting.

THE VALUE OF MENTORSHIP

Mentoring is one of those things we all need, whether we realize it or not. Having a mentor allows you to learn things you would not otherwise learn about your profession, because there are some things that simply cannot be put in a textbook or employee handbook. Even if you are the top dog in your organization, you need a mentor. Someone who formerly held your position or a more experienced peer working in another company can serve as your mentor. Don't be shy. Ask them to be your mentor. Most people will be flattered and honored to have the job.

A mentor is someone who:

· Provides on-the-spot training for receiving constructive criticism, performance evaluations, and advice.
· Saves you from developing bad work habits that might otherwise go unnoticed until they are a problem.
· Kick-starts your network of business professionals.
· Teaches you how to interact with people in positions of authority and seniority.
· Teaches you how to converse and interact with professionals in your industry.
· Makes it easier for you to understand and adapt to the culture in your workplace or profession in general.
· Confidence and competence come to you more readily because you have someone guiding and (re) directing you as you go.

In addition to having a mentor of your own, you need to *be* a mentor, too. Some of you may think that coaching is mentoring; so since you are coaching your employees, you assume you have that covered. But coaching and mentoring are two different things...sort of.

Coaching is training someone to create their own success story in their job by adapting to and thriving in the culture of the workplace. Mentoring is different in that it is more personalized and intense. It is a grooming and preparation for passing the proverbial torch. But for all the good you do when you mentor someone, you reap plenty of benefits, too.

- Mentoring takes you out of your comfort zone of assuming people know what to do, when to do it, and why it needs to be done.
- Mentoring allows you to give back to your profession.
- Mentoring reenergizes your career mindset.
- Mentoring gives you the feeling of satisfaction that comes from helping someone.
- Mentoring (re)teaches you to be an active listener instead of a passive listener.
- Mentoring forces you to look beyond your immediate responsibilities and see the business or organization as a whole, and that everyone plays a vital role in its overall success.

Not only does mentoring serve to build relationships; mentoring benefits a business by:

- Portraying the business as one that believes in investing in their employees.
- Portraying the business as one that believes in its future.
- Creating a positive work environment and a sense of trust and cooperation among everyone no matter where they are in the chain of command.
- Fostering leadership skills.
- Developing a sense of loyalty among employees.

In my opinion, mentoring is the best investment you can make in the future of your business.

PAY YOURSELF FIRST

I know that over the years, a lot of business gurus have said that starting and owning your own business requires you to pay yourself last—if at all—until the business is fluid. I'm here to tell you this is not the way it should be done. And believe it or not, I'm not the only one saying that.

More and more people are realizing that it is OK to pay yourself first under most circumstances. There are several reasons why paying yourself first is a sound business practice. Among those reasons are:

- You still have to eat, too.
- When you pay yourself at least a portion of what you should earn for all your hard work, you feel more successful. And when you feel successful, you are successful.
- Paying yourself first is a strong motivator to work harder to increase the amount of money your business brings in. In other words, if you know you have to make X amount of money in order to get paid, you'll hustle to make X amount of money.
- Paying yourself first is a smart tax move.

When deciding how much to pay yourself, you will obviously need to take a few things into consideration such as:

- What is the bare minimum I can get by on? This is all you should pay yourself to start.
- Do I really need it? Some people prepare for opening a business by saving enough money to live on for six months, so if you don't need it and can put it back into the business—for example, paying for inventory, paying down a loan, and so on—then by all means do so.

The rule of paying yourself first is just like every other

rule—there are exceptions to it. Some of these exceptions include:

- Don't pay yourself first if you cannot pay your staff.
- Don't pay yourself first if you cannot meet other financial obligations with the business (loan payment, paying vendors, etc.).

RECOGNIZE WHEN YOU ARE ON THE RIGHT TRACK

Tony Robbins, in case you didn't know, is one of the world's leading experts on leadership and strategies for building a successful business. I have learned several things from him over the years, but I have to say that one of the most profound statements he has made—or at least the one that resonates with me the most—is, "Success leaves clues."

That statement is simple, yet so powerful. As business owners, we can see for ourselves if we're on the right track. Of course, the money thing is a telltale sign, but money isn't everything—not even in business.

So what are some of the other clues you need to look for to know whether or not you are on the right track with your business?

- Client loyalty. They aren't coming back just because

you happen to be close by. People will go out of their way for great customer service.

- Client recommendations. If new clients are referrals from current clients, you are at the top of your game.
- Low staff turnover. In 2017, not one single stylist quit their job at Fox and Jane in New York City. That's impressive for any business, but in the salon industry, that's pretty much an unprecedented miracle.
- You show up at or near the top of the page on an online search (search engine optimization). A strong and prominent online presence speaks volumes.
- You garner the attention of the media—in a good way, of course. FYI, it is perfectly acceptable to offer your business up as a subject to be highlighted in a small business profile article.
- You don't have to be there in order for things to run smoothly.
- You don't feel like you have to bend or compromise your culture to please a client.

When it comes to owning and operating a business, you have to listen to your gut, which is your logical train of thought; not your heart, which is ruled by your emotions. The *feelings* you have about your business aren't what really matters. What matters is what you *think* and *know* about your business.

IT'S YOUR TURN

THE BUSINESS OF BEING IN BUSINESS

———

1. Why are you in business? What brought you to this profession?

2. What is the mission statement for your business? FYI, if you don't already have one, you are about to get one.

3. What are some of the changes you have seen in your business since you first opened the doors?

4. What has been the best change?

5. What has been the worst change?

6. What steps do you take to stay in the know regarding your industry—the trends, obstacles, economic issues, technological advancements, opportunities, and so forth?

7. How aware are you of what is going on in *your* business?

8. What measures do you have in place to track the financial health of your business without being a micromanager?

9. How readily can you state each employee's strengths and weaknesses?

10. How well are you using these strengths and weaknesses to determine where each employee is placed in your business? Are they being allowed to be an asset to the company, which in turn gives them the opportunity to grow to their full potential?

11. When you make decisions about promotions, are you doing so based on what you *know* from observing and interacting with the candidates? Or are you basing your decisions on hearsay and faceless applications and résumés?

12. Who are the people in your business network? Use the space below to write their names, their areas of expertise, and what they have done to positively influence and affect you and your business.

A. _____

B. _____

C. _____

D. _____

E. _____

F. _____

G. _____

H. _____

I. _____

J. _____

K. _____

L. _____

M. _____

N. _____

O. _____

13. Order each of the following according to its importance in regard to running a successful business. (Begin with the most important and end with the least important.)

    A. Competent and confident employees.
    B. A website that is up to date, easy to navigate, and easy to find.
    C. Your commitment to being a positive and active presence in your community.
    D. Genuine relationships with your employees that go beyond what they do on the job (in an appropriate fashion).
    E. Networking with other business owners in the community.
    F. Networking with other business owners in your industry.
    G. Social media presence.
    H. Being in the know about everything that goes on in your business—from a business standpoint.
    I. Using a coach approach to leadership.
    J. Training leaders you can trust to colead your business to success.

14. Who are your mentors?

15. Why do you consider these people your mentors?

16. Who are you mentoring? Why?

17. Let's take another look at the benefits of mentoring from various perspectives. Next to each one, give an example of how you have realized this in your life and in your business.

- Mentoring takes you out of your comfort zone of assuming people know what to do, when to do it, and why it needs to be done.

- Mentoring allows you to give back to your profession.

- Mentoring reenergizes your career mindset.

- Mentoring gives you the feeling of satisfaction that comes from helping someone.

- Mentoring (re)teaches you to be an active listener instead of a passive listener.

- Mentoring forces you to look beyond your immediate responsibilities and see the business or organization as a whole and how everyone plays a vital role in its overall success.

- Portrays the business as one that believes in investing in its employees.

- Portrays the business as one that believes in its future.

- Creates a positive work environment and a sense of trust and cooperation among everyone no matter where they are in the chain of command.

- Fosters leadership skills.

- Develops a sense of loyalty among employees.

18. Reread the section on "Paying Yourself First." Do you agree or disagree with what you read? Why?

19. How does your model for earning an income from your business differ from this?

20. Are you on the right track? Use this page to think on paper. Write down the pluses and minuses of being in business: what you would like to change, what you are proud to say is working well, and what you would like to see happen in the future. When you are done, take a few minutes to read it—carefully. Let it soak in. Allow yourself the luxury of dreaming big.

Now go make those dreams come true!